SUPERLOVE

Superlove

A Guide to Happiness in Personal Relationships

Anne Naylor

Thorsons
An Imprint of HarperCollinsPublishers

Thorsons
An Imprint of HarperCollins*Publishers*
77–85 Fulham Palace Road,
Hammersmith, London W6 8JB
1160 Battery Street
San Francisco, California 94111–1213

Published by Thorsons 1993
1 3 5 7 9 10 8 6 4 2

A catalogue record for this book
is available from the British Library

ISBN 0 7225 2821 3

Phototypeset by Harper Phototypesetters Limited,
Northampton, England
Printed in Great Britain by
HarperCollinsManufacturing Glasgow

To Ma and Pa
from whom I have always received love.

Contents

Index of Exercises   11
Introduction   13

Self-Acceptance . . . The Relationship with Yourself   19
  Happiness Statements   19
  The Relationship with Yourself **(I)**   20
    Self-Awareness   21
    Accepting the Facts   25
      Your Willingness to Love Yourself **(I)**   25
      Out of the Ordinary   28
    Changing your Way of Thinking   30
      Guidelines for Making Affirmations   30
  Developing the Relationship with Yourself **(I)**   33
    Inspirational Self   34
    Inner Child   36
    Love in your Relationships **(O)**   40
    The Will to Effect Change **(I)**   41
    Taking Action   43
    Caring for Yourself   45

Understanding . . . Personal Accountability and
Co-operation   47
    The Relationship Scientist   48
  Accepting 'Inner Rocks' and Blind Spots   49
    Learn from the Rocks   51
  Relationships as Bridges   56

Language – Meaning and Misunderstanding   61
Resolving Conflicts from the Inside Out   62
Bring in the Light   65
Understanding your Inner Child (I)   67
The Triangle of Trust   68
The Higher Perspective   71
Understanding – An Intuitive Response   75
Act or React – The Choice is Yours   76
The Power of Positive Digestion   79

Peace . . . Becoming a Friend to Yourself (I)
and Others (O)   83
Cultivate Positive Peace   85
Receiving your Peace   90
The Peace Cycle   90
1. Acceptance   91
2. Co-operation   92
3. Understanding   93
4. Peace   94
Riding the Rough Terrain   95
Peace, Perfect Peace   99
Exploring Guilt and Resentment   99
Forget – or Regret   104
Re-writing the Intention in your Heart   107
From Distance to Intimacy (I)   110
Growing from Grief to Gratitude   113
Listening – A Key to the Door of your Peace   114

Expansion . . . Winning in All Ways   116
Your Journey Outwards   116
Abandon your 'Rights' (O) and
Go for the Value (I)   117
The First Steps   118
Consider your Options   120
Learning, Healing and Integration   123
Beyond the Shadow of a Doubt   124

Doubt – The Way Out to Expansion   126
  1. Nurturing   127
  2. Discipline   133
Forgive – and Be Blessed   134
The Path of Perfect Parenthood   137
Authentic Relationship   138
  Choosing the Positive Option   140
  Sacrificing the Negative   141
  3. Fun   144
  Lighten your Load with Laughter   147
  Expansion is Fun   147
  Keeping a Light Touch   148

Rejoice . . . It's a Wonderful Life   150
  Accepting the Value and Role of your Feelings   150
    Early Trading and Negotiation   150
    Denial of Feelings   151
    A Loving Reminder . . .   153
    Imagination – It's Child's Play   154
    Reclaiming the Dream   158
  Guardian Angels of your Growth (Listeners)   164
    The Realm of Magic and Surprises   167
    Waking the Sleeping Giant of Intuition   172
    Acts of Loving **(I)** + **(O)**   176
    Set the Children Free   179

Love . . . Life in All its Forms   180
  Self-Acceptance . . . The Relationship with
Yourself **(I)**   181
  Understanding . . . Personal Accountability and
Co-operation   184
    Look with Loving   187
  Peace . . . Becoming a Friend to Yourself **(I)**
and Others **(O)**   188
    Peace that Grows from the Inside **(I)** Out **(O)**   190
  Expansion . . . Winning in All Ways   191

Expansion – The Path of Least Resistance   192
Expanding through Effective Communication   193
Rejoice . . . It's a Wonderful Life   193
Walking Blessings   196

Index   201

Index of Exercises

Self-Acceptance

Self-Acceptance – The First Steps   23
Accepting a Positive Orientation   26
Your Hero   29
Attuning to your Inspirational Self   34
Relating with your Inner Child   37
Happiness – The Journey that you Make   42
Happiness – What is it for You?   43
Taking Good Care of Yourself   45

Understanding

Understanding – The First Steps   50
The Friendly Rock Reveals Its Truth   54
Building the Inner Bridge   58
Listen, Learn and Re-direct   63
Switch Up!   66
Learning How to Love your Inner Child   70
Taking a View from Above   73
Dear Inspirational Self . . .   78
Caring and Compassion – Digestive Enzymes   81

Peace

What is Peace for Me?   84
Recognizing the Gifts in Camouflaged Wrapping   86
Breathing In – Breathing Out: It's your Peace   92
Dismantling your Barricades   96

Liberation from Guilt and Resentment 101
Forgiving Yourself **(I)** 105
Statements of Forgiveness 109
Receiving your Peace 111

Expansion
Knowing What You Want **(I)** 121
Vulnerability – Your Key to Creativity 129
Clearing the Way with Forgiving 135
Laying Down the Positive Track 142
Learn to Say 'Stop' 143
Nurturing the Sparkle of Delight 145

Rejoice
Create a Day of Magic 155
Dreaming the Dream 159
Preparing a Fairy Godparent Charter 166
Treatfeast 170
Entertaining the Divine Within You 173
    Your Cosmic Joke 176
Your Garment of Invincible Clothing 177

Love
Loving Observation – The Key to the Door of
your Happiness 182
Turn on the Light of your Understanding 186
Understanding – with the Eyes of Loving 187
Peace – Gratefully Receiving the Gift of your Life 189
Give **(O)** – and Receive **(I)** your Peace 191
Your Gift from the Child Within 195

Introduction

Superlove: A Guide to Happiness in Personal Relationships is an approach that will lead you to enriching yourself and to bringing lasting pleasure in your relationships with others.

It is about achieving significant improvements in current and future relationships through cultivating peace of mind and contentment in the relationship with yourself. Within you is an extraordinary potential for extending greater kindness and compassion towards yourself. In turn, this will enable you to bring ease, harmony and fulfilment in all your relationships, whether or not you are currently having problems with a teenager, mother-in-law, noisy neighbour, employer, teacher, politician or the tax man.

The solid foundation for *Superlove* is self-acceptance and learning to love those aspects of yourself that in the past you may have rejected or denied. In order to more fully accept yourself and successfully grow in your relationships, you will need to see, without shame or blame, who you are. Learning how each and every relationship can serve you, not sabotage you, is only one of the outstanding rewards of personal accountability – the ability to recognize that others reflect to us those aspects of ourselves which we may have yet to accept.

The language of personal accountability is expansive, emotionally neutral and can be seen in words such as 'assessment', 'discernment', 'evaluation', 'observation' and 'could'. The limiting language of negative emotions can sometimes be recognized in words such as 'judgement', 'critical', 'should', 'fault', 'blame' and 'shame'. Awareness of the language you use can alone reveal adjustments you can make for increased happiness.

The exercises and examples in each chapter are fun, practical and easy to do. They will generate experiences of loving that lead you to new understanding and remarkable freedom in your interactions with others. It is when we are out of alignment within ourselves, experiencing emotional conflict such as self-doubt, guilt, resentment or loneliness that we need to pay attention to, and love, the 'Inner Child'. When confronting a difficulty, we can gain access to, and receive from, our own personal resources of wisdom and guidance, represented here as the 'Inspirational Self'.

In this way of resolving our inner conflicts, producing increased happiness, we can become an intimate friend to ourselves, extending only the clarity and strength of loving into our relationships. By perceiving more of our innate goodness, we may also perceive the loving qualities in others and achieve extraordinary rewards in this adventure of learning to express and experience the power of loving in our lives.

Superlove will make you see your life through fresh eyes. There may be ideas, new to you, that can radically transform your life. So have fun experimenting with an open mind to discover more fully the creative resources of your own capacity for loving. Above all, in exploring relationships with this guide, be gentle, patient and caring towards yourself. Small steps taken over a period of time will produce the greatest results.

Superlove is not about short-lived romance. It will enable you to attract and create long-term relationships that will be most supportive, nurturing and enjoyable. Treat *Superlove* as a friendly companion to give you a helping hand in resolving your relationship difficulties, in gracefully releasing those that no longer serve or support you, and in establishing new, happy relationships that will make a very real difference to your enjoyment of life as a whole.

Happiness is like a butterfly: if you try to pursue it, it will elude you. While you are actively engaged in, and enchanted by, your own pursuits, it will come and sit softly on your shoulder.

Chapter 1

Self-Acceptance

. . . The Relationship with Yourself

Happiness Statements

Consider the following statements concerning **Happiness**.

♥ We can *contribute* towards the happiness of others, but not be finally accountable, or responsible, for it **(O)**.
♥ We *are*, however, ultimately responsible for our own happiness **(I)**.
♥ We can be happy even when those close to us are unhappy (we are then in a better position to contribute to their happiness if we wish) **(I) > (O)**.
♥ If you want to be happy, contribute towards someone else's happiness **(O) > (I)**.

You may not immediately agree with all of these statements, but bear them in mind and we will consider them more fully later.

   If you are wishing to get more out of your relationships, it is highly probable that you will need to change part of your outlook or behaviour. This is where you may confront challenges to your familiar patterns and habits. The exercises in *Superlove* are offered as an opportunity to actively explore and experiment with approaches that may be different for you and subsequently lead to insights that will improve the quality of your life experience. They are designed to assist you to find what you may already know, but have lost from conscious view. Only by doing them can you expect to gain any benefit from them. You may find it fun and effective to do them on occasions with a friend whom you trust to support your emerging strengths and with whom you feel safe.

To begin, let's consider your primary relationship . . .

The Relationship with Yourself (I)

Culturally, many of us have been conditioned to believe that a 'relationship with ourselves' is selfish, narcissistic and anti-social. However, to effectively 'know yourself', you do need to get in touch with those deeper aspects of yourself that may be concealed from you in the course of your everyday activities.

The relationship with yourself then, in its most factual and basic sense, is the bridge between you, the observer, and the responses of your feelings, emotions, thoughts and physical body.

The following points illustrate this a little further:

1. You are the only one who can truly know what gives you pleasure and what causes you pain. If you are hurting, it is up to you to make the first move to heal the hurt (which may involve asking for assistance and support from others).
2. When you are lovingly in charge of your inner environment, you will be less inclined to blame and punish someone else (possibly the one you love the most) when you experience upset or disturbance. With this self-awareness, you become master of your inner household and can restore your inner harmony and balance as needed without expecting someone else to 'make you better'.

3. The care that you show to yourself tends to be reflected back in the loving that others close to you show you. As you become more responsible for how you feel, you will not be projecting anger out to someone else and your outer relationships will then be easier and more direct.

4. Similarly, as you take steps to create your own happiness, you will have positive qualities to give to others – i.e. as you gain greater attunement within yourself **(I)**, you will be guided inwardly to enrich the relationships that you have with others **(O)**.

Self-Awareness

The relationship with yourself begins with the first step of *self-awareness*. This is important. From self-awareness, you can then move to *self-acceptance*, the basis for rewarding relationships.

You may be aware of a prayer that goes along the lines of:

> God grant me
> the *courage* to change what I can
> the *serenity* to accept what I cannot change
> the *wisdom* to know the difference.

In this next exercise, you will have an opportunity to review characteristics and qualities in yourself that you do not like. Some may be those with which you were born and which are essentially unchangeable, such as body build and height, skin texture and colour, sex or sexual orientation, facial features, race and cultural inheritance, your age today, talents and aptitudes – or perceived lack of them. We may judge ourselves against standards and images that we assume as being acceptable and worthwhile in the world around us, such as a certain body type: 'Slim is beautiful' (and in the eye of the beholder?); youthfulness:

'Young people have everything to live for' (what about the wisdom of a lifetime's experience?); sex: 'It's a man's world' (is it?); or race: 'Whites are superior' (are they?) Peer pressure, advertisements and the role models presented by the media lead us to believe that a clearly defined physical image is the way to be happy. You may feel yourself judged worthwhile, or otherwise, *as a person* because of the way you look.

The first guideline of this 'Guide to Happiness in Personal Relationships' is that of directing loving kindness, caring and compassion *towards yourself* to attain self-acceptance. For some of us, self-acceptance may be the work of a lifetime because we may have buried patterns and habits of self-rejection, self-denial and self-sabotage far from our conscious awareness. Years of self-rejection cannot be immediately turned into self-acceptance like an instant cake mix.

The effective approach to adopt is a steady and gradual one, taken with patience and whatever time is required for the changes to take place. What may seem slow at first will in the longer term prove to bring about the most lasting benefit. If by the end of the chapter you have not yet worked the miracle of your own self-acceptance, the following chapters will continue to reinforce it. The insights you gain from reading *Superlove* and doing the exercises may take as long as two years to become fully a part of your everyday life. Two years is the usual length of time for a new way of life to become established as a working pattern.

Self-Acceptance – The First Steps

For this exercise, you will need a pen and paper. Bring to mind those characteristics about yourself that you do not like and list them. You might reflect on physical characteristics first of all, then think about personality traits, patterns of behaviour or habits that you dislike.

For example:

1. My face is ugly.
2. I don't spend enough time with the kids.
3. I am lazy and put off doing things.
4. I hate my skin colour.
5. I am always late for appointments.
6. My stomach is too ,fat.
7. I am too short.
8. I lose my temper a lot.
9. I am really stupid when it comes to doing my accounts.
10. I am a failure.

The task with those dislikes is to review them in a more objective and emotionally neutral way and then to restate them as a detached observer. You might imagine yourself as a visitor from another planet, having no preconceptions about what may be the prevailing standard or image against which you have been judging yourself. Rewrite your list now as an observing extra-terrestrial.

For example:

1. I have an interesting and unusual face with strong features and gentle eyes.
2. My life is very full at the moment and I spend as much time as I can with the kids.
3. I sometimes put off doing things I am not really interested in doing.
4. My skin has a fine and beautiful tone.
5. I am a spontaneous person who enjoys life and I sometimes find I get absorbed in what I am doing and end up arriving late for meetings.

6. I have a rounded tummy like a teddy bear.
7. I am 5 feet 4 inches tall.
8. I have a quick mind and strong emotions so sometimes I explode rather like a firework when my touch paper is set alight.
9. Numeracy and handling figures are not my strong talents.
10. I am a person who learns through my experiences of life.

With this last list, you may notice self-acceptance appearing within you, something like an inner calm, rather like the stillness of a deep lake as against the turbulence of ocean swells which might toss and turn you, mentally and emotionally.

Now reconsider your first list. There is an important distinction to be made between the characteristics which you cannot change and those which you could, potentially. Looking at the examples above:

2. You could spend more time with the kids (if you chose to).
3. You could organize yourself to get things done (if you wished).
5. You could retrain yourself to be on time (with practice).
6. You could eat less and take more exercise (for a fitter physique).
8. You could learn to be more patient and relaxed (with loving).

If you truly wanted to effect those changes and were willing to take the action necessary to do so, you could achieve those results and probably enhance your relationships with others as well.

The best starting point for initiating new attitudes and behaviour is that of self-acceptance, without guilt or shame. The greater challenge for self-acceptance concerns those facts about yourself which you cannot change.

Now, having read through the exercise, get a pen and paper and have a go at doing it yourself. You may be pleasantly surprised at how it turns out.

Accepting the Facts

Learning to accept that which you cannot change may be one of the greatest challenges in your life. You cannot change the fact that you are tall or short, pink-skinned or brown-skinned, that each day your body is growing older and taking shape accordingly. You may have been born with the challenges of little, or no, sight or hearing; defective limbs or other body conditions.

Not accepting, or rejecting, the facts is rather like hitting your head against a brick wall that is right in front of you. It hurts. When you direct the force of your mind and emotions against the condition you interpret as unacceptable, you are similarly inflicting pain on yourself (I). That pain which you are creating inside will also find its way into, and undermine, your relationships with others (O).

Alternatively, as you accept the facts without any negative reactions, you will automatically have more of your energy available to enjoy your life. Not only that, but in so far as you accept yourself, others will also – and even if you do occasionally receive negative responses from others, they can bounce off you because you are in a frame of self-acceptance.

Your Willingness to Love Yourself (I)

The first recipient of your Superlove is going to be you.

This may not be what you wanted to read. The fact remains.

The first step in loving yourself is that of freely accepting who you are. This is far from narcissistic, as you need to be able to accept not just that which you approve of, but also some of those facts about yourself that you do not like and which are not within your power to change. As mentioned before, if you reject or deny any of your features or characteristics (I), then you have a weak foundation for loving others (O).

Rather than fight the unchangeable facts about yourself,

you can accept and *co-operate* with them – even turning your 'disadvantages' into 'advantages'. You may be aware of people with obvious physical disabilities who nevertheless lead extraordinary lives. Why not you, with whatever 'disabilities' you may have perceived about yourself?

In this next exercise, you will be using any unchangeable characteristic you have identified which you have not yet fully accepted. When you can accept that there may be a constructive purpose for you behind a characteristic, it will be easier to accept it.

Accepting a Positive Orientation

What is the characteristic about yourself which you cannot change and have not yet accepted? It might be some feature of your body, your level of intelligence or academic ability, your age or anything that you consider unlovable about yourself.

For this exercise you will be drawing that characteristic in symbol form. You do not have to be a good artist – only you need recognize what the symbol represents for you. Put pen or pencil to paper and just allow the form to appear.

When you have completed this, write out any feelings or emotions that come to mind as you look at the drawing. You may feel sad or angry. Keep writing down your thoughts and feelings until they are out of your system. On no account reread what you have written. The idea here is to release the negativity, not to dwell in it.

Next, tear up, burn or destroy, however you wish, both the symbol and your emotional description.

Now spontaneously draw a symbol representing the positive orientation that that particular characteristic holds for you. Do not think too much about it, as this may prevent you from drawing anything at all. Allow your pen or pencil to do the 'thinking' for you as you draw. Afterwards, you can observe the positive message that symbol has for you. Then, in one statement preferably, describe its constructive purpose for you.

The examples below illustrate how this exercise can look.

If you have just been reading through this, now have some fun and do it for yourself.

Figure 1: 'Negative' characteristic.
Beanpole. I am too tall. People hated me at school. I don't like
being called lanky. I always get noticed. I hate being tall. I want to
be short. Why did God make me this way?

Figure 2: Positive interpretation.
I am a sunny person and my height lets me extend my warmth to
lots of people so I have many friends.

Out of the Ordinary

You may be feeling yourself to be a special case, with the facts or conditions with which you were born. The personal challenges with which you were endowed may seem to go beyond the limits of your tolerance. The fact, for example, that you are black and therefore at the receiving end of discrimination, or that you are now too old, or infertile, to bear children. Don't despair! Non-acceptance of a fact works like a poison in your system, eating away at your vitality. An antidote for such poison is to be found in the many examples of people who, with seemingly unsurmountable obstacles, lead out of the ordinary lives: the blind black singer who has not only achieved success in his professional field but has also gained respect for his humanitarian deeds; the elderly nun who devotes her life to caring for the untouchables, diseased and aged in the city streets. You may be aware of the lives of extraordinary people close to you who are an inspiration and serve to put your own 'facts' into a different perspective.

The energy which you may have directed against yourself as a 'poison' may alternatively be used creatively to accept the facts and lift the inner quality of your life to a new height. The circumstances of your life, and how you choose to address them, may well be 'out of the ordinary'. What you have in common with everyone else is essential human energy.

This next exercise is one in which you can begin to awaken your own powers of creativity in taking the next steps towards self-acceptance.

Your Hero

The first part of this exercise is to state the fact which you find unacceptable and write out all the ways it prevents you from having a good life. This could include things like lack of mobility, isolation from others, problems with getting employment, communication difficulties. By simply stating the conditions that surround a fact and writing them down, you are taking a step back from them.

Now take a few moments to reflect on people you consider to be extraordinary. These people could be living or dead, literary characters, humanitarian leaders, or individuals within your own neighbourhood or community. You might also consider those who have or had obvious physical obstacles or conditions with which to live – the best-selling author who tapped out a novel with one toe, for example.

Whoever it is that comes into your mind, jot down the qualities that you experience that person demonstrating. These might be qualities like endurance, compassion, resourcefulness or courage. What are those qualities that you observe in your heroes or heroines?

Now, select at least three of those qualities and consider the following points:

1. You recognized those qualities because you already have them within you.
2. The qualities you identified are those that will assist you to accept your 'unacceptable' facts, and enable you to lift the inner quality of your life to a new height.

If you have only read through this exercise, you cannot expect to benefit from it. This 'Guide to Happiness in Personal Relationships' is only another set of good ideas until you put them into action in your life. Do the exercise now!

Changing your Way of Thinking

As well as 'unacceptable' facts about yourself, you may have patterns of thinking and behaviour that reflect self-rejection. Analysing those patterns and trying to work out where they came from does not necessarily make them go away. In order to achieve self-acceptance, you will need to assume the patterns of thinking and behaviour that *demonstrate* self-acceptance.

It seems as though we each of us have a certain predisposition to attract specific people, events and life conditions that reflect aspects of our make-up. Up to a point, we are the victim of who we are. We do not, however, have to live with the attitude of a victim.

How you both perceive, and experience, yourself does give you scope for improvement because you are capable of changing your thoughts and feelings. In order to arrive at where you would like to be (say, greater happiness and freedom) you need to know where you are now. Suppose you were flying to Brazil, for example, it would help to know whether your starting point was Rome or Fiji. Your *direction*, and your methods of transport, would be different in each case, depending perhaps on the terrain you were crossing and the transport available.

One of the simplest, most effective ways of creating a new set of internal conditions or expectations for ourselves is to affirm the experience *as if* it was already a reality right now. This technique is simple and yet profound. If it is new to you, use the following guidelines from my previous book, *Superlife*, to assist you in experimenting with it.

Guidelines for Making Affirmations

1. Each affirmation is stated positively, with no negatives, so that each word of the affirmation has a positive image for you.
   For example:

'I never get angry when my son has rock music on loud.'

Although there is a positive idea here, it is stated negatively. It is better stated:

'I love my son enough to ask him to turn the music down when I get home tired from work.'

2. Each affirmation must be stated clearly, and be something that you can imagine for yourself and that you really want.
   For example:

   'I expect to be strong when I meet my boss tomorrow.'

would be better expressed as:

   'I am clear and confident of achieving my winning objectives with my boss.'

3. To be most effective, an affirmation is stated in the first person, present tense. First person because the only person whose thinking and behaviour you can change is yourself. Present tense because you are introducing the new thought pattern right now, and again, the only time at which you have any control is now.
   For example:

   'My secretary will produce this letter perfectly.'

is not a useful affirmation, for as much as you would like you really cannot determine your secretary's attitudes and behaviour in the future. So it would be better to phrase this as:

   'I am giving my secretary the support she needs to be an excellent member of our team.'

4. Use words that stimulate and inspire you into the

strengths and qualities you want to have more fully in your life. Let your imagination run free here – an affirmation is only for you.

For example:

'I am determined.'

An affirmation like this, simply stated, can be powerful and effective. However, you could experiment with expanding the statement with more colour and flair so that your inner attention is called fully into play:

'With ease, confidence and enthusiasm, I am persistent and purposeful, valuing myself as I courageously take each step towards my success.'

Do not be concerned if your affirmations (or other people's) sound odd or funny, especially if they produce the results *you* would like.

5. Choose affirmations that match your priorities. Make sure that they are in line with your overall picture. Take care to limit the number you use at any one time. Like any other agreement you undertake, make sure that your affirmation pledge is one which you will want to follow through and complete.

These outlines are a basis for the technique. Feel free to explore and discover how they can most effectively work for you.

Here are some examples that will illustrate the technique. You might like to adopt, or adapt, them for your own use. Choose no more than three to work with for a period of, say, a month so that you can observe the changes taking place within you.

- ♥ I am strong, courageous and powerful.
- ♥ I enjoy being me.
- ♥ I am clear, decisive and wise in my thoughts, words and actions.'
- ♥ When I wake up in the morning, I am relaxed and happy.
- ♥ I accept, love and appreciate myself.
- ♥ I take care to maintain a healthy balance in my life.
- ♥ I am loving in my full and enriching friendships.
- ♥ I am an excellent listener.
- ♥ I treasure my vulnerability and sensitivity.
- ♥ I express myself clearly, with humour and trust.
- ♥ I am true to myself and communicate with honesty and love.
- ♥ It is fun for me to make my life easy.
- ♥ I enjoy being enthusiastic and effective.
- ♥ I love and respect myself, just as I am.
- ♥ My mind is positively focused, filling my life with harmony, balance and well-being.
- ♥ I look at the world in a positive light and envisage the best possible outcomes in everything I do.
- ♥ I take on only that which I can fulfil with ease and grace.
- ♥ I have pleasure in using my gifts and qualities to the full.
- ♥ When life is challenging for me, I bring forward my greatest strengths.
- ♥ I transform my 'blocks' into blessings.
- ♥ I am treating all problems as opportunities to grow in wisdom and love.

Developing the Relationship with Yourself (I)

In order to develop the relationship with yourself, you will have the opportunity to explore two of the aspects that make up who you are. These are your:

1. Inspirational Self.

2. Inner Child.

To look more closely at those aspects of yourself:

The Inspirational Self

is like an inner guide or wise counsellor. In order to make contact with this resource, you may need to take a break from the bustle and distraction of your normal activity. The Inspirational Self may be that 'still small voice' that gives you words of wisdom in a calm moment. When you can take time out to go for a walk, for example, or relax in a warm bath, you may find you receive the insights you need to resolve an issue or concern. Some forms of meditation are also a good way of gaining access to your Inspirational Self.

In this next exercise, a guided visualization, you will have the opportunity to use your creative imagination and envisage your Inspirational Self as a wise friend. This may be the best way for you to make contact with this higher aspect of yourself.

Attuning to your Inspirational Self

There are several ways of doing a guided visualization, so use whichever is the best for you. Here are some suggestions:

1. Record the entire visualization on cassette so you can listen to it all with your eyes closed, inwardly reflecting.
2. Read through the visualization, paragraph by paragraph, closing your eyes at the end of each to reflect on its contents.
3. Ask a friend to read through it for you as you do it.

As this is a process of inner attunement, you will get the most out of this exercise by making time for it in which you will be undisturbed by the telephone or other distractions. You may find that having some soft music in the background assists you to relax and tune inwardly.

Take in a few deep breaths, and, as you let those out, let any tensions in your body ease . . . Be aware of any feelings . . . and let them go . . . Notice if there are any thoughts in your mind . . . Watch them pass like clouds crossing a blue sky on a warm summer day . . .

Imagine yourself enjoying a sunny day . . . in a beautiful place in the countryside . . . or on a beach . . . or in a forest . . . on a hill . . . or in a meadow . . . wherever is best for you . . . Feel the warmth of the sun on your skin . . . a cool breeze gently caressing you . . . see the brightness of the colours . . . notice any movement around you . . . leaves . . . blades of grass . . . flowers . . . the ocean waves . . . birds . . . or animals . . . Hear the sounds of your scene . . . wind in the trees . . . birdsong . . . the splash of water . . . the crunch of gravel beneath your feet . . . Experience the happy vitality all around you . . .

Envisage yourself getting up and exploring this exuberant world . . . Look at it with different eyes . . . and notice now what you discover about it . . . Imagine yourself running through this scene . . . and experience your sense of joy permeating and filling you . . .

Find a quiet place . . . sit down and make yourself comfortable . . . When you look up you notice a friendly and in a strange way familiar figure standing by your side . . . You indicate to this person to sit beside you . . . and feel the warmth of affection and love that is present for you . . .

Your friend takes your hand and you can feel this warmth extend throughout you as you listen to the words, 'I am always with you. I am here to love and support you now.'

As you receive these words, you experience a deep sense of reassurance . . . a profound peace fills and surrounds you totally in a way that you have never known before . . . When you look once again towards your friend . . . you become aware that both of you are within a radiantly clear white light . . . and you notice that some of the darkness that was previously in your consciousness is now being lifted from you . . . as though this light were a magical cleaning agent of great power and gentleness . . .

As this light seems to be growing brighter . . . you notice that your *friend has a gift for you . . . You open your hands to receive it . . . and explore the package . . . How is it wrapped? How large is it? Is it light or heavy? What do you think might be inside it? With a sense of excitement, you remove the wrapping . . .*

What do you discover inside? Describe it to yourself in as much detail as you can . . .the colour . . . the size . . . the shape . . . the feel . . . texture . . . sound . . . warmth . . . coolness . . . What does this gift mean for you? How can you use it to enhance the relationship with yourself?

Your friend is now standing up . . . and assisting you to your feet . . . You thank this special person for the gift . . . and share a warm embrace . . . with a squeeze of your hand . . . you are reminded that you are loved . . . that you have a special place in your friend's heart . . . and now once again you are on your own . . . but filled with loving . . .

Very gently now, gradually return your attention to the world around you . . . While these good feelings are still present in your consciousness . . . take a few minutes to make any notes about your experience . . . especially about your gift and its meaning for you.

Finally, complete the following statement in any way that is nurturing and uplifting for you:

'My Inspirational Self is . . .'

If this is a technique that is new for you and perhaps seems strange, treat it as a gentle experiment in exploring your inner worlds of loving. It does not take very long, so do it now.

The Inner Child
is your source of energy, vitality and the inner world of your feelings and emotions. A good relationship with your Inner Child will also improve the experience of your power and sexuality.

When you feel fear, anger or any other emotional upset,

you may find that your Inner Child is out of balance and, in its own way, demanding your attention. Negative emotions serve a valuable purpose when you recognize that they can be attention-getting devices.

Often, beneath an upset, is a justifiable reason for it. For instance, self-rejection is felt deeply by your Inner Child and may cause him or her to be rebellious, uncooperative or otherwise 'childish'. Self-criticism, and feelings of guilt and shame are ways in which we reject the Inner Child. So, for example, if you have the good intention of going on a diet but at the same time hate or punish yourself for some reason, the Inner Child may well sabotage your new nutritional programme.

Throughout *Superlove* you will have opportunities to learn how to love your Inner Child and experience the 'child-like' qualities of fun, enthusiasm and creativity, which are available to you at any age. To obtain the best results from this book, you will be inviting the co-operation of your Inner Child. Rather like a child that is upset, your Inner Child needs to be heard uncritically by a friendly ear. Chapter 5, 'Rejoice', is dedicated to the Child within us all.

A good way of establishing contact with your Inner Child is through a dialogue writing exercise, in which your conversation slows down to make time for your responses. This next exercise provides the opportunity to allow the emotional side of your nature, as your Inner Child, to express whatever is on his or her mind.

Relating with your Inner Child

You will need a pad of paper, a pen and an open mind to get the feel of this exercise. Allow yourself about ten minutes when you know you will be undisturbed.

You can physically locate the Inner Child in your body as the area around your naval. Placing your hand over that part of your abdomen is a way of making contact with the Inner Child. Do that now. You may feel a sense of reassurance and comfort. It may help to close your eyes for a moment, so that you can take your attention inwards. Take in a few deep breaths and as you let each one go, allow yourself to become more relaxed.

Do not be concerned if this seems strange for you at first. Treat it as an experiment and allow yourself to be as spontaneous as possible.

In the dialogue you are about to have with your Inner Child, you might like to write an initial for your name, say 'A' for Alan and write your Child's name as Little Alan, 'LA'. Listen uncritically to your Child as a caring friend. Listening carefully is the primary purpose of the exercise, for as you become a good listener to yourself **(I)**, you will also be developing this skill for use in your relationships with others **(O)**.

Below is an example which illustrates how your dialogue might turn out. It is just an example, not the only right way to do this exercise. Your dialogue could look very different in content – much shorter or longer – so do not feel inhibited by however your Child wishes to communicate. Be aware of whatever you can learn from your own dialogue. A seemingly insignificant detail may be instrumental in giving you a fresh outlook in a challenging situation.

A: How are things with you today?

LA: I am feeling fine.

A: Would you be willing to do this exercise with me?

LA: In front of all those people?

A: It will probably be only one reader at a time.

LA: OK then. What would you like me to say?

A: Yesterday I was feeling very nervous and irritable. Can you tell me something about that, for example?

LA: Yes. Actually you took care of me pretty well.

A: Thank you. But what was happening with the 'nervous and irritable'?

LA: I was feeling sad and disappointed underneath.

A: What were you feeling sad and disappointed about?

LA: Not everything is going the way I would like and I feel frustrated that I do not know how I can change it for the better.

A: Oh, I think I understand. You know what? I think we may just have to be a little more patient. It may take a little more time before either we know how to change the situation or allow the circumstances to evolve. I apologize if I set up a false expectation with you.

LA: Well, OK.

A: Does that feel any better now?

LA: Yes. Actually, I did feel better yesterday when you took some time to relax and go out for a walk. Listening to that music was also soothing.

A: Is there anything else you would like to tell me about?

LA: Not now. We probably have another exercise like this later on, don't we?

A: I think it is very likely.

LA: I will save up what I have for the next time.

A: Fine with me. I love you very much.

LA: I love you too – most of the time.

Put aside any feelings of reluctance and give yourself the opportunity of getting in touch with your Inner Child with this exercise now. Your dialogue may turn out differently from the example above, so feel free to find out how it will work best for you. Give yourself and your Inner Child permission to explore this simple format. You may find it very rewarding.

An important consideration to bear in mind is not only that the source of your upsets can often be pin-pointed and resolved through the Inner Child, but that as you direct positive reinforcement towards yourself, you will awaken the joyful and expansive qualities within you. Practising a greater positive orientation may take discipline if your Child has absorbed a lot of negative input in life so far, but the rewards may prove well worth the effort.

Negative orientation would include limiting attitudes and beliefs – tending, for example, to view certain people and life events as problems rather than as opportunities. Positive orientation embraces grief and sadness with compassion, without dwelling in them and projecting more misery into the situation.

The Child within you sees the potential joy and humour in almost any 'disaster' you will encounter. He or she will welcome any opportunity you can provide to play, have fun and celebrate your life. Along these lines, consider the people and situations that upset you. You could, with the Child's awareness, make them lighter – and preferably select more of those that are fun and nurturing for you.

Love in your Relationships (O)

Your basic drive in relationships with others **(O)** springs from the following deeply felt desire:

I want to love, and be loved **(I)**.

When you give and receive love in an active and dynamic form, it is also true to say that:

To love, and be loved, produces happiness.

The potential of greater loving in our lives is a very powerful motivator. You may not yet know how to express your love most effectively or how to be open to its experience. However, through learning how to accept yourself and your loving resources **(I)**, and to co-operate better with them as you relate to others **(O)**, you will enhance your relationships.

Most of us would like to feel that we can predict and control the course of our lives. The notion that we can do this may give us a sense of security in an uncertain world.

However, you can never truly control another person, and if you try, you will limit the potential for happiness in that relationship.

You may be familiar with the following saying, which has been attributed to several people:

If you want to change your world, who do you start with?
Yourself, or other people?

Your 'world' includes other people. But in order to improve your relationships, you cannot change *them*. You must make the changes within *yourself*.

The Will to Effect Change (I)

As the greatest scope for change and improvement in any relationship is going to be within yourself, *your choice* of attitude and actions, the commitment you make, is going to be, first and foremost, *to yourself* **(I)**. Your will-power can really only function effectively on a foundation of clearly wanting and valuing yourself enough to achieve a more positive experience for yourself. And, as already mentioned, *only you can know what you want*, however much anyone else tries to tell you what you 'should' want.

The following exercise is a goal you may wish to nurture for yourself through the course of the book. It uses the affirmation technique described above (*see* pages 30–3).

Happiness – The Journey that You Make

. . . not the Destination

Start as you mean to go on. First of all, recall a time, an incident or an event in which you experienced happiness. Cast your mind over your life so far and become aware of one such moment. Were you radiantly happy and surrounded by others who shared your happiness? Or were you quietly alone, enjoying a precious interlude just being with yourself, perhaps with some music, a beautiful scene from nature, a favourite pet animal?

Recall now all the details of that experience. Notice colours, textures, sounds, any other feelings you had, recreating it all vividly in your imagination as if it were occurring right now in this instant. When you are fully immersed, take in a deep breath and, as you let that breath out, say to yourself:

'I AM HAPPY.'

Take in a few more *I am happy* deep breaths and observe your feelings of happiness expanding.

You may wish to experiment creatively with how you use this affirmation. Below are some suggestions that you may wish to adopt or, better still, adapt or use as starters for yourself.

♥ If you are feeling tense or upset, stop what you are doing and practise some *I am happy* deep breaths until you feel calmer and more relaxed.

♥ Write *I am happy* on your bookmark as you read through this book.

♥ Write *I am happy* on the next ten pages in your diary so you will see it each day.

♥ Make up an *I am happy* song and sing it to yourself in the bath, shower or car, when you are driving to work.

♥ Repeat *I am happy* three times to yourself last thing at night before you go to sleep and first thing in the morning as you wake up.

♥ Repeat *I am happy* as you do five minutes of jumping jacks . . .

and remember:

> Do not take life too seriously.
> You will never get out of it alive.

Taking Action

Affirmations alone are not going to effect the improvements you would like to have. In addition, you need to take the *constructive action* that reflects and reinforces the quality of experience you would like.

You may have already found that when you reflect on a subject, it is amazing what you know about it beyond a superficial level. Take happiness as an example in the next exercise.

Happiness – What is it for You?

In this exercise, you will need a pen and paper to explore the following statements for yourself. Allow yourself to do this exercise very spontaneously. No one else has to read what you have written so give yourself permission to be free to express whatever comes to mind. There are no 'right' or 'wrong' answers to the questions.

Write down the opening words and complete the statements at least five times, or as often as possible.

1. Happiness is . . .
2. I am happy when I . . .
3. A happy moment was when . . .

For example:

1. Happiness is a warm bath.
   Happiness is waking up after a good night's sleep.
   Happiness is walking on new mown grass.
   Happiness is getting my own way.
   Happiness is great sex.

2. I am happy when I make people laugh.
   I am happy when I dance.
   I am happy when I listen to upbeat music.
   I am happy when I do my meditation.
   I am happy when I give my lover a massage.
3. A happy moment was when I received a silver cup for winning
   a swimming race.
   A happy moment was when I got up to talk in front of a large
   group for the first time.
   A happy moment was when I rode a jet ski on a Mexican bay.
   A happy moment was when I smelt cedar wood for the first time.
   A happy moment was when I gave a carrot to my favourite horse.

Were any of the statements that came to mind in some way
'unacceptable' to you? You may be one of those who knows full well
what evokes happiness in you, but has been told in the past that
'good' people don't do or think those things. If that has been so for
you, you might just be aware of it for now.

   You may have found that even thinking about happiness has now
caused you to feel happier. You could also have found that you
experienced sadness. Either way, simply observe any responses you
may have had.

   Simple steps to promote happiness in yourself and others can be
profoundly effective. So now select three actions you will complete
in the next week:

1. To promote happiness within yourself **(I)**.
2. To promote happiness in relationship with a loved one **(O)**.
3. To promote happiness in the outer world **(O)**.

For example:

1. Take a day off to go to a health farm for a day of massage.
2. Prepare a special surprise candlelit dinner for my spouse.
3. Sell ten books of raffle tickets for the school swimming pool fund.

Make a note of how you experienced this part of the exercise.

Caring for Yourself

In the sometimes challenging arena of personal relationships, it is important that you do take good care of yourself. The following exercise will assist you in making an important move into increased self-acceptance.

Taking Good Care of Yourself

The task is to agree three actions that you will complete within a week that perhaps you have been meaning to do for a while, and that will be nurturing for you.

Write down in a list the actions you want to take. Make these very specific and easy to fulfil in the time suggested. Also write in the time when you will complete them, such as Friday afternoon or Tuesday evening.

For example:

1. Take an afternoon to go for a long walk in the fresh air.   By Wednesday night.
2. Buy the Vivaldi CD I have been wanting for ages.   By Saturday afternoon.
3. Book a weekend retreat in the Tibetan monastery.   By the end of today.

To complete the exercise, check back in a week's time, and review the following questions:

1. Did you complete your assignments?
   If so, was that easy for you?
   How did you feel having completed them?
   What benefits did you experience?
2. If you did not complete them, what was the reason?
   How did you feel about not completing them (be honest here)?
   What did you learn about yourself from this exercise?
   What did you learn about your choices and actions?

This exercise is an important one for several reasons. Any time you agree to do something, you unconsciously prepare and marshall your energy to bring about the completed result. When you fail to follow through on any commitment, you let yourself down. This is a form of self-rejection which leads to self-doubt, low self-esteem and unhappiness.

This is especially true if the agreement you have made is specifically *for yourself*. We often get so busy doing things for other people that we forget that we ourselves need attention and nurturing.

If you have a pattern of promising that you will do something for yourself **(I)**, such as give up smoking or undertaking a fitness programme, and do not fulfil those promises, you may find that in your relationships, other people do not keep their commitments to you **(O)**. You will find that often your disagreements with *others* are telling you something about a disagreement *within yourself*. When you point one finger of accusation towards another person, you might notice that three fingers point back towards yourself.

The lesson here is that you only ever undertake that which you clearly intend to fulfil. Learning to care for yourself and not to let yourself down is a fundamental way of achieving a happier frame of mind. You can consciously choose to replace self-defeating habits or patterns of behaviour with more constructive, loving and productive actions.

Do the exercise now, and when you have completed it in a week's time, give yourself a treat or reward. You can never be too good to yourself.

As you come to accept the various aspects of your human nature you will come to discover the generous stream of goodness that is sustaining your life. All the conditions, positive or negative, inner or outer, that you may encounter can be viewed as opportunities to awaken you to more of your qualities of happiness and freedom. Self-acceptance is the foundation of a happy life well lived.

Chapter 2

Understanding

. . . Personal Accountability and Co-operation

The foundation of self-acceptance gives you the confidence to gain greater understanding (I) in your relationships (O). Understanding is not something we can hope to work out with our minds alone. All the intellectual explanations in the world do not necessarily 'teach' us to do better the next time. Emotionally, we often repeat the same mistakes.

Young children are often asking the question 'Why?' as they learn and come to terms with the workings of the world around them. The question 'Why?' is sometimes better answered as if it were 'How?' For example, 'Why does water come out of the tap?' is best explained by allowing the child to turn the tap and discover what happens. The child *understands by experience* how action A produces result B. No amount of rational explanation or mental reasoning can enable this learning to take place.

Similarly, as adults, in our quest for greater loving and happiness in our relationships, we may hear ourselves asking the question 'Why?' concerning an experience we do not understand. The question 'Why?' sometimes implies a subtle level of self-criticism, as in 'Why did I get fired?' or 'Why did he walk out on me?' or 'Why do I feel so lonely?' So the question 'Why?', with its implication that we did something 'wrong' or, worse still, that we may be a 'bad' person, does not lead us towards understanding what we might do in the future to have more loving in our lives.

The Relationship Scientist

This chapter will explore understanding from the 'how' perspective, examining relationships as if you were a scientist observing what happens.

Consider the following equations:

Decision **(I)** + Action **(O)** = Experience **(I)** + Result **(O)**
Experience + Loving = UNDERSTANDING

It is important to recognize that there is an absence of criticism here. Increasing *self-acceptance* is an aspect of gaining understanding. You will simply have the opportunity to discover *how* your thoughts, speech and actions produce certain outcomes – which you may then either like or dislike.

As a scientist, you may wish to conduct experiments **(I)** in your relationships with others **(O)** to break out of self-defeating habits or patterns and act creatively on some new decisions or choices. No experiment or experience need be wasted or regarded as a 'mistake'. In inventing the light bulb, so the story goes, Edison made 1,000 attempts in his progress towards his final understanding and the product we recognize as 'light bulb'.

We may occasionally switch on understanding, much like a light. Often, however, we may need several attempts before we get the lesson within an event that leads to the light of our understanding. First and foremost, we need to exercise patience, especially towards ourselves **(I)**, as we gradually utilize more of the loving in our lives.

Understanding then is within us **(I)**. It grows through our loving relationships with others **(O)**. Any relationship experience we have had, whether we have interpreted it as positive or as negative, is potentially a springboard to our understanding and wisdom.

Accepting 'Inner Rocks' and Blind Spots

In the same way as we have physical features to accept about ourselves, we also have mental, emotional and personality conditions that we need to recognize and accept as our own. It may not be until we respond (I) to another person (O) that we discover some of the 'rocks' and blind spots on our path. The clues here will be in our negative reactions to the behaviour, attitudes, actions and even mannerisms that we see in others. *How we react* (I) will be telling us much more about ourselves than the other person.

Our reaction is usually not an inner response to what we look at *objectively*, but to *how we perceive* what we see. To illustrate this, describe what you see before you now. It might be the details of furniture in the room, the colours of the fabric, possibly a window with a view. Now if you were to turn around to face exactly the opposite direction and were to describe in detail your present location as you *now* see it, you could have another accurate description which is completely different from the first. Two people looking in different directions are likely to have not only different views, but also different perceptions of those views.

In the following exercise, you will have the opportunity to discover, this time perhaps as a 'relationship scientist', how you are at the mercy of your own rocks and blind spots. As you become aware of them and accept them as being part of your own human make-up, you may relate to them more as assets, and less as liabilities, in your relationships.

Understanding – The First Steps

First of all, bring to mind anyone who evokes a strong negative reaction in you, someone who disturbs your inner calm and equilibrium. This could be a person – your mother, step-father, son-in-law, step-daughter, employer, politician, religious leader, television personality, teacher, civil servant, successful entrepreneur – or a group of people – hippies, yuppies, and so on.

Write down the name of the person, or the type, and describe how and why they are distasteful to you. Feel free to write down in as much detail as possible all of their faults and failings. You may feel quite angry, self-righteous and resentful as you do so and that is fine. Keep on writing until you have got them totally summed up. For example:

> ### Son-in-law – Edward
> *Edward is a drip. He is bright but he never makes an effort. He'll never get a job. Other candidates always have more going for them so he never gets picked. He did not get any qualifications so he'll never be any more than an administrator. At best. He is just useless. I can't see what Sally ever saw in him in the first place. Why doesn't he get up and do something with his life instead of just hanging around like a lemon . . . etc.*

Your description is a set of undesirable qualities and characteristics that you have objectively recognized in another person or type of person. But in each statement of your description is a rock or blind spot *of your own* which you have yet to accept. It may not match word for word, but there will be an essential similarity that you can come to recognize as being within you. You may not always find the match. Sometimes these rocks and blind spots remain unconscious because the pain associated with them is not yet ready to be revealed and healed.

The next part of the exercise will be effective in so far as you can extend towards yourself an attitude of acceptance and the willingness to have human frailties. Write a description of yourself in which you see the negative characteristics you previously attributed to your *bête noire*.

For example:

The 'Me' I see in Edward

I feel useless some of the time. I am capable but I have never really met my potential. I feel lethargic sometimes and as though I am not going anywhere in my life. I could have done much better. My former classmates have been much more successful than me.

Now you might be able to understand that in order to improve your perception of, or relationship with, another person **(O)**, you need to extend a loving acceptance towards yourself **(I)** and, if necessary, your shortcomings, whatever they are. If you misunderstand yourself **(I)**, you project misunderstanding **(O)**; if you have hate inside yourself **(I)**, you put hate out towards someone else. So in order to allow others to be free in relationship to you **(O)**, you need to be free within yourself **(I)**.

This exercise could be an important step towards your freedom and happiness – do it now.

Learn from the Rocks

The active healing of former hurts and disappointments can provide a bridge within yourself **(I)** to your own inner resources, the resources which enable you to enjoy increased enrichment with others **(O)**.

Look at the patterns of thinking and behaviour you have based on old hurts or disappointments. Hurt may tell you, 'Don't go in that area, it is painful.' Well, maybe it was once, when you were unequipped to know how to deal with it. An extreme example would be that of child abuse: when, as an adult, you would like some of the benefits of feeling close with one or more others, the price you seem to have to pay looks high. So you may well transmit mixed messages which end up sounding something like 'Get away closer' and the result is not oneness but stress.

So how can an inner rock of residual *hurt* be transformed into a stepping stone towards *intimacy*?

Imagine for a moment that hurt is represented by darkness, a lack of knowing and understanding. You might open a door into a room that was completely dark. If there were furniture or other obstacles within the room, you could not see them. You might feel your way around, but be unsure of what you might touch. Your imagination might become reckless in producing a lot of fear, the fear of the unknown. What if you chanced to touch a light switch? The room which represented so much fear could now be flooded with light so that you could see and, if you wished, relate with its contents, possibly exploring them a little more closely and seeing them for what they are. You might also be able to find the door and your way out whenever you chose. You might also recognize the door when it appears in your consciousness, and choose not to go into that room now you are familiar with it.

When you can become aware of a *pattern* of inner response to certain – usually unpleasant – outer events in a relationship, you may realize that you have just stumbled into an old piece of furniture in the dark room. Although it is *your* piece of furniture, you may feel as though other people have put it there, and therefore *they* are to blame when you stub your toe. In a sense of course, they are. However, they are truly offering you the chance of understanding the rocks in your consciousness. With awareness, you might be more grateful than angry at their participation in your evolution.

Then how, in the moment of upset, can you step back sufficiently to gain the awareness and insight being made available to you? How can you switch on the light of your consciousness to move out of conflict and into understanding?

They say that opportunity only knocks once. The remarkable thing is that patterns repeat themselves over and over until we do learn from them. When you bruise yourself on a piece of furniture, you might curse the furniture and whoever you thought put it in your way. Alternatively, you could also accept it, sit on it and explore how it feels, as if you were an objective scientist getting to know the material in your laboratory, and recover. There is nothing intrinsically wrong with the material. It's just that you may not yet have learnt how to utilize it in the best, most fulfilling, way for yourself.

The following are some options you may have already explored in attempting to understand your rocks. Disappointments such as the lover who left you, the child that went off the rails in spite of all the sacrifices you made, the premature death of a parent may leave a rock wall inside of us, with the aim of protecting us from a similar hurt in the future. In a way, those rocks serve a purpose and may remain solid until we expand inwardly to embrace them with our increased capacity for loving.

1. **Analysis**
   You may analyse your rocks, explore the reasons for their existence and become therefore familiar with them. In this way, you may temporarily disassociate yourself from the pain, but not dissolve it. You could even find someone else to blame for it, but that disempowers you from healing the hurt.
2. **Emotional involvement**
   You may also re-evoke the feelings and emotions concerning former hurts and disappointments, reliving them vividly as if there were once again part of your present experience of life. But emotionally recalling the past does not necessarily lead to the understanding that frees you from it.

3. Denial

You may push the rock to the back of your mind – and yet it nevertheless seems to follow you around. It may become visible in other people, even though it has 'nothing to do with you'.

When you are ready to do so, another possibility is to relate to your rock as the relationship scientist. Instead of applying your faculties of analysis and reason or stirring up old emotional grief, you may simply accept the existence of the rock with a relaxed frame of mind. Acceptance allows a space for reflection and new insights to come into view. Relate with your rock as an observer. Sit on it. Observe your responses to it. Experience how it feels for you.

When you are ready to do so, allow your rocks to reveal their truth to you. You may find, as the saying goes, that the truth sets you free. All that has been previously hidden from you is a gem that you would have paid any price to receive. See what insights you can gain from the following exercise.

The Friendly Rock Reveals its Truth

Your feelings are an important source of information when you can *observe* them and not be *dominated* by them. This is a 'feelings awareness' exercise in which you can explore an issue or an upset with a degree of objectivity. Just imagine you could graduate from university with a Degree of Objectivity. That could prove a really useful qualification.

It is important that you can be honest or, in a sense, at one with yourself. In subtle ways, you may make others the cause of your upsets and in that case you cannot resolve them for yourself. Putting your rocks in someone else's court does not discharge them from you.

First of all, to get the idea of how this exercise works, bring to mind a significant upset that you experienced some time in the past and recall it as if it were happening right now. Make a note of the event and run the following questions through your mind. Write down your responses to the questions:

1. How do I feel in myself?
2. How do I feel about the circumstances and what is happening? *(Be specific.)*
3. What *is* happening? *(Take an objective, neutral view.)*
4. How can I relate more effectively *(i.e. lovingly)* with

a. myself?
b. the other person/people?

The answers might look like:

It was the summer term of three years ago. I had to stay at home to revise for exams and everyone else went out for the day.

1. I feel sad and lonely.
2. I feel cross that I was left behind and I resent having to work to get any qualifications.
3. I am at home revising for my exams and the rest of the family have gone to the beach for the day.
4. I can relate more lovingly . . .

a. with myself by taking a break to stretch my legs and get some fresh air every so often.
b. with the rest of the family by welcoming them back home with a warm hug later on.

The next time you experience yourself feeling upset, run these questions through your mind and gain some objectivity for yourself. Bear in mind that we always potentially have a choice as to *how* we react to anyone outside ourselves. As long as we blame someone else for how we feel, we disempower ourselves. The remedy for any hurt feelings or upset is always a loving one.

Pain is often an informer. It may come as a messenger, laden with news from the battlefield of your inner conflicts. You may be in your fortress, reluctant perhaps to hear the news, possibly fearing the worst. When you are ready to lift the barriers to your awareness, it is rather like surrendering a filter that you have held against yourself **(I)**. That which was a filter to your perception becomes a doorway through to clarity in your relationships with others **(O)**, a bridge of understanding.

Relationships as Bridges

Relationships offer us a bridge between our essential aloneness **(I)**, and the oneness we can experience with others **(O)**. What then are the stones, timber or metal structures that go to make up our bridges? What action can we take to build a greater connectedness with those we love and care for?

1. **Communication**
   - we can listen to what others have to say to us about their wishes, needs, cares and concerns, keeping an open, uncritical frame of mind in which they are free to express their truth without fear of losing our love and respect
   - we can express our own wishes, needs, cares and concerns openly, without making the listener the cause of how we are experiencing ourselves inwardly, so that we remain accountable and responsible for our feelings and thoughts
   - based on the above, we may negotiate outcomes that serve the greatest good for all concerned
2. **Physically touching**, as appropriate

- warmth communicated through our hands to another person can bridge many gulfs that words, with their occasional misinterpretation, fail to do
- touching, when it is an extension from the warmth you have within you towards another person, is often irresistible
- touching may become inappropriate if it is inflictive, manipulative or motivated by some 'hidden agenda'

3. Inner contact

- since the relationship with others **(O)** is founded on the relationship we have with them inside of ourselves **(I)**, we can make contact inwardly and communicate the love we have for them through a 'heart' connection

To expand on that last idea, the realm of our feelings, thoughts and emotions is *within ourselves*. We may feel ourselves to be *a victim* of others' behaviour and opinions a great deal in our relationships, and that may be, in the main, how we have learnt relationships to be. But you will come to discover that you are responsible for how you experience yourself **(I)** in any relationship with another person **(O)**.

It is true that you may not always be able to communicate loving to another person outwardly. You may be in the midst of a disagreement about something, there may be hostility between you or the person may be physically in another location, for example. But if you are inwardly churning resentment towards another person, the one who suffers most will be you.

An option that is always available to you is to build a bridge *within yourself* to meet your adversary and to clearly communicate the loving intention that you have for the relationship.

What is the non-material outcome that you would like to experience with that other person? We sometimes expect that other people should come over to our point of view, but it is precisely these expectations that lead to our disappointments and hurt feelings. If we want something to change, we have to make the first move. We may not be able to envisage the method **(O)** by which we can come to an agreement, but we can potentially envisage the experience that we would like to be enjoying with the other person *within ourselves* **(I)**. As we focus positively on the inner qualities that we already have at our disposal, we may get some insights as to how we can relate more effectively and express our loving outwardly. Then some patience may be needed and some time allowed for the healing to take place.

In order to enrich a present relationship, we can learn from previous experiences of disappointments or hurt feelings. The following exercise is one in which you can heal a relationship memory from the past which may make for ease, pleasure and fulfilment in present and future relationships.

Building the Inner Bridge

Bring to your mind a conflict, disappointment or hurt feelings that you experienced in a relationship a while ago. It could have been in your childhood, with an ex-spouse, a close friend or business associate. You might have felt let down, abandoned, abused, betrayed, humiliated, rejected or otherwise misunderstood.

This exercise is in the form of a guided visualization. As before, have a pen and paper by your side for any notes you would like to make after you have taken the inner journey. Minimize any possible disturbances so that you can take the next few minutes quietly for yourself. Take the phone off the hook, close the door if necessary and put any distractions to one side.

Take a few deep breaths . . . and as you let them out . . . allow yourself to become more relaxed and peaceful inside . . . As you reflect inwardly . . . just imagine yourself being filled . . . surrounded . . . and protected by a very clear white light . . . This light is here to bless . . . and to heal you . . . from any past memory or hurt . . . so that you can now enjoy the quality of your life more fully than ever before . . .

Bring into your conscious awareness the loving you have within you . . . It might be through recalling the love you have for a child . . . your spouse . . . a pet animal . . . a piece of music . . . or a scene in nature . . . Ask yourself inwardly for this loving to guide you now . . . as you expand beyond former limiting experiences . . . experiences which can now be released from your memory patterns . . . to make way for understanding and freedom in your relationships from now on . . .

Recall an upset that you experienced in a relationship . . . a disturbance that occurred with someone you valued and cared for . . . or whose approval and respect was important for you . . . Bring a specific incident to mind . . . with as much detail as possible . . . so that you can imagine it unfolding right now . . . What was being said . . .? Or not said . . .? What were the attitudes . . . gestures . . . expressions . . . facial features . . .? What was the true source of the upset or disagreement . . .? What was your point of view . . .? How did you justify your position . . .? To yourself . . .? To the other person . . .?

Let that scene fade from view . . . Take in a couple of deep breaths . . . and as you let them out . . . let your shoulders drop . . . and allow your body to release any tension that it may have been holding . . .

Imagine now that you are standing on one side of a river . . . It might be a small stream . . . or a wide estuary . . . or anything in between . . . Between you and the other side is a bridge . . . At the far side is standing the person with whom you experienced disappointment or hurt feelings . . . Notice the structure of the bridge . . . Is it made of ropes . . . steel girders . . . stones . . .? Does it look very solid . . .? Or is it flexible to allow for the movement of wind . . . or heat . . .? How does it span the water . . .? High up . . . or close to it . . .? Is it suspended or supported by columns . . .?

Envisage yourself stepping on to the bridge . . . and notice how firm it feels beneath your feet . . . Even if the wind seems to move it a little, you are confident that it will support you as you cross over it . . . See yourself walking along it until you arrive at the mid-way point . . . Feel the exhilaration as you watch the water flowing beneath you . . . and as you look towards the other person . . . notice his/her qualities of warmth and contentment . . .

As you continue along the second half of the bridge . . . you feel lighter and freer . . . There is a quality of enthusiasm bubbling through you as you come closer to the person on the other side . . . With that inner sense of fullness . . . you greet the person . . . smile . . . reach out to shake hands . . . or share a hug . . . The loving that you now extend towards the other person is being expanded within you as his/her loving comes back to you . . .

If there is anything you would like to express verbally, you can do that now . . . You might also listen for anything that person would like to say to you . . . Be open and receptive . . . What is it that you can hear now . . .? Does it lead you into a consciousness of acceptance and understanding . . .? Experience the quality of peace as it revitalizes all the cells of your body . . .

With that peaceful feeling radiant within you, bring your attention back to where you are now . . . gradually . . . and in your own time . . .

Make any notes that you would now like about that experience, especially any understanding that you received concerning your relationships with others.

Recall the structure of the bridge you crossed. What were the qualities within you that it represented? For example, steel girders might be your integrity, ropes your inner flexibility.

Bring to mind the water you were crossing. What challenges does it represent to you in your relationships with others? For example, fast-moving water might be the emotions that sometimes get you in difficulty, a broad river the distance at which you sometimes keep yourself from others.

This is an exercise that you can do to overcome and release regrets from the past. See how you can use any of the insights you received to enrich yourself in relation to others.

Language – Meaning and Misunderstanding

Language too can be a bridge – it is the most effective way of achieving intimacy and endearment with another. The misuse of language, however, can prolong conflict. It may be true to say that words will often misrepresent our finest feelings, which can never be adequately expressed verbally. How can we ever truly describe the love we experience for a child, the moment of watching a sunset, or, more crucially perhaps, our deepest hurts?

The way in which we can lessen verbal misunderstandings is to become more accurate in our use of language. When you can make the distinction, for example, between hard fact and emotionally backed opinion, both in what you hear and in the words you speak, your communication will become more effective.

Use the following summary of common 'blind spots' to become first of all more accurate in your own speech. If we fall into these 'communication traps', we may be misleading others **(O)**, intentionally or otherwise. More importantly, we may be deceiving ourselves **(I)**. This self-deceit can lead to misunderstandings.

Communication Blind Spots

1. **Distortion** – emphasizing for the sake of drama or winning someone's attention.
2. **Deletion** – being 'economical with the truth'.
3. **Generalization** – making sweeping, often judgemental, general statements.
4. **Interpretation** – drawing personal conclusions from a set of facts.

5. **Opinion** – taking a view based upon a personal perception.
6. **Speculation** – anticipating a future outcome from a current interpretation of events.
7. **Projection** – assuming the future will match our experiences from the past.

Once you are aware of what to look out for, as you listen to others or read what they have written, check for accuracy. In this way you may become more aware of the meaning that is being communicated beyond the words. That meaning is often an expression of the fundamental desire, mentioned before:

I want to love, and be loved.

Resolving Conflicts from the Inside Out

When you witness, either in yourself **(I)** or in one or more others **(O)**, the expression of anger, resentment or even violence, it is likely to be coming from the experience of hurt or pain. Understanding and extending kindness and compassion, firstly towards your own areas of hurt **(I)**, will ease any discords you might have with others **(O)**.

Typically, we hurt when we fail to accept that life is not the way we want. This includes those we love! Out of our sense of empathy, we may also feel hurt by the pain we witness **(I)** in others and judge the world **(O)**, and even its Creator, as being unfair. This hurt, the refusal to accept either the way life is or our inability to change it, may be projected out from us in forms of anger or pushed down inside us to produce depression. Either way, we have set up an inner conflict.

The following is an exercise to practise on a conflict within yourself, a hurt that you are essentially containing.

Although it may have been based on a disagreement triggered by someone else **(O)**, you will be examining your *own* responses and reactions to it **(I)**.

Listen, Learn and Redirect

In this exercise you will have the opportunity to evaluate how you can use the energy available to you to serve you more productively or effectively. Following on from this, personal energy that is being consumed 'negatively' may be released and made available for you to use to enjoy your life more fully.

Recall a conflict you experienced in the past and imagine it is happening right now. The more recent the conflict the better, for the more immediately you can address the moment of upset and lessen the memory of it the better in terms of achieving a resolution for yourself.

There are three simple steps here:

1. **Listen**
   Stop, and watch what is happening *within* you. You might find it helpful to make some notes on paper to assist you.
2. **Learn**
   What was the trigger – **(I)** or **(O)** – that initiated this negative emotional reaction?
   At what point did you **(I)** allow or promote or create the upset?
   How could you have responded differently? (Explore, if you can, three possible alternatives.)
3. **Redirect**
   In order to 'reclaim' your energy, the final step of directing yourself – taking action – will assist in liberating it, and you with it.

Redirection may involve focusing your attention on something which interests and absorbs you, or on something that perhaps makes you feel calm, peaceful and happy. Directing your energy into a physical activity is one of the best ways of releasing a negative build up inside yourself and returning to greater equilibrium. Walking, running and swimming come into this category, if time presents itself. Cleaning a car, housework or gardening are other productive uses of this energy.

Gaining self-awareness enables you to become more the cause, and less the effect, of what happens in your relationships. You can then choose ways of relating to others that best support you and enable you to be more loving.

For example:

When I was away for a couple of days, a friend borrowed my iron and did not return it. When I came back home, I needed to use it and discovered it had gone. I got angry and resentful towards her, firstly for not asking if she could borrow it and secondly for not returning it.

1. **Listen**

   I was feeling angry and resentful that I was not consulted. I was also angry with myself because the issue was a small one but nevertheless irritating and inconvenient. I heard myself voicing my anger towards my friend but then feeling guilty because perhaps her need was greater than mine. The issue seemed to ricochet around in my head for quite a long time. What probably made it worse was that I was tense from my travelling and in the mood to see things negatively.

2. **Learn**

   The trigger that initiated the negative emotional reaction was discovering that the iron was not in its usual place. Then inside myself **(I)** I felt let down and almost 'abused', as if my property had been 'stolen'.

   I made the upset worse by assuming that the iron had been taken and not returned as an act 'against' me, that someone was out to sabotage me. I cannot remember 'at what point' exactly and was not aware of this specific reaction until I thought about it right now. But I could have responded differently by:

1. Being more loving towards myself and in a relaxed frame of mind when I came home.

2. As there was no immediate urgency for the iron, I could have phoned at a convenient time and asked her to return it.

3. I could have asked her to tell me in future if she wanted to borrow any of my property. I could have used this opportunity to build greater trust with her instead of feeling negative towards her.

3. **Redirect**

   What I did was to phone later and go and collect the iron myself so that the situation was resolved. However, if I had been in a calmer mood, I could also have been more receptive to her needs **(O)**, felt less like a 'self-righteous tyrant' – the criticism I levelled *against myself* **(I)** – and been more forgiving towards myself **(I)** for having reacted in a way that was less than loving.

It is important that you do the exercise for yourself, allowing a spontaneous response to each stage of *Listen, Learn and Redirect*, without feeling you have to come up with the same answers as in the example. You might find that the example is a guide if you get stuck, but as far as possible discover what is true for you. You will probably find that you have many more choices available to you than you had at first considered.

Bring in the Light

Remember that light switch. You can lift heaviness and darkness of negative emotions by turning your attention to something more positive. Your own sense of humour, enjoyment or fun can switch on your inner light.

The following exercise will give you a mini-break from any misunderstandings as they occur. If you find that this mini-break works well for you, you might take one more often.

Switch Up!

This exercise is a quick-fix to practise when you want to lift yourself out of a potential inner conflict **(I)**. It can lead you to greater understanding of an issue. Primarily it will give you a rest from the conflict and return you to a warmer contact inside yourself. Warmth can relax you and release your creative, problem-solving resources.

For the purpose of finding out how this exercise works, recall the most recent incident in which you found yourself stuck in the middle of dark emotions (anger, fear, guilt, resentment, depression or simply a bad mood). Envisage yourself there now in as much detail as possible. Imagine yourself in the location and, if there were any, with the other people concerned in this experience. See, hear and feel yourself in the seriousness of it all. Do not allow yourself to be aware of any humour entering into the situation.

Now identify the positive emotion you would most like to be experiencing. It could be happiness, kindness, joy, fun, vitality, spontaneity. Fix the emotion as a thought in your head. You could see it written across your forehead in gold letters or a bright light, you might feel it in the centre of your chest, you could hear it being whispered in your ear or being shouted from a mountaintop.

To shake loose the negative emotions, do something physically right now to switch that positive emotion up into all the cells of your body. You could get up and stretch, take in a few deep breaths, jump up and down on the spot and repeat that quality – preferably out loud with a full voice or at least inwardly as you move. Just do it for a couple of minutes. If you can think of something funny and laugh at the same time, so much the better.

This may seem ridiculous to you but before you dismiss it, have a go and do it. You could be amazed how simple it is to 'switch up' and change your perspective from one of limitation to one of expansion and understanding.

This example will assist you to see how it works:

The situation I am bringing to mind is one in which I feel a combination of irritation, anger and depression about not knowing how to balance the tasks I have set for myself with the other areas of my life which are important to me. I also feel both self-righteous and too serious.

The positive emotion I would now like to be experiencing more fully is fun. I can see the letters FUN written inside my forehead. In my imagination I can shrink them and see them bubbling around my bloodstream, infusing all my muscles, skin, bones, internal organs with fun. The effect is somewhat ticklish. When I go out to do my errands, I shall keep focusing on that quality of fun as it fills me, and notice how the world responds to me.

I will put on some really 'up' music and dance for a couple of minutes.

The two parts of the exercise must be done to achieve the full result of 'switching up'. The first is an inward change **(I)**. Inwardly you are in charge of your own emotional control panel. The second is an active change, translating the thought into activity **(I) > (O)**. A third, if opportunity presents itself subsequently, is to express or communicate in some way that quality to one or more others **(O)**. Sometimes it is not until you give of your qualities that you discover you have them.

If you find that you later allow your energy to sink back into the former negative emotion, consciously make the effort to 'switch up' to the new choice. You could even imagine yourself flicking a light switch as you do so.

To conclude the exercise, you might like to make a note of how you experienced doing both parts of it. This could be a useful reference for you in the future.

Understanding your Inner Child (I)

Accepting and co-operating with circumstances that may be beyond your immediate control rests largely with the level of co-operation you have inwardly with your Inner Child

(I). When you can anticipate potential difficulties in your relationships with others as being 'opportunities' or 'challenges', you are offering a positive framework into which the Inner Child can direct his or her energies. The capacity for successfully managing yourself **(I)** in your relationships **(O)** is based on a foundation of trust with the Inner Child.

The Triangle of Trust
Consider the following *Triangle of Trust*:

1. **Nurturing**
   Never underestimate your needs at any age or stage of life for tenderness, caring and loving attention. Here is the kind of understanding that you can extend under the most testing of circumstances. Patience, tolerance and acceptance of your vulnerability in what is not always an easy and accommodating world will keep you in touch with the creative resources of your Inner Child.

2. **Discipline**
   Clear agreements and parameters that respect your personal boundaries, and are agreed with the Inner Child, enable you to enjoy a quality of freedom in your personal relationships. Those around you need to know what is important for you in relation to them. This is not a matter of building walls to keep others out, but more one of letting them know the direction that is going to enable you to give the best of yourself.

   Keeping to the agreements you make with yourself in your relationships will measurably enhance the quality of your life as a whole.

3. **Fun**
   Nothing rewards the Inner Child so much as creative play. So remember to give yourself a break. The spark of glee kept alive within you will assist you in creating and

maintaining the kind of inner resource state that empowers you in any relationship. It is hard to strike out at one who is in contact with their sense of humour. Laugh, and the world laughs with you.

The following exercise is an opportunity to put into practice the above points. There is a skill in knowing when to nurture, when to exercise discipline and when to allow free-form, spontaneous, even outrageous, play in adult life. Your Child has many wonderful resources but needs your clear direction as to appropriate timing sometimes. While you are developing this relationship of greater co-operation, remember that *your* idea of appropriate timing may not coincide with your Child's.

You could also bear in mind that your Child has much to learn and therefore is likely to make mistakes. Perhaps your real education in life only begins when you leave your formal schooling. How you relate with your Inner Child in the course of learning will affect how well your 'tests' are conducted and passed.

You may recognize non-cooperation in your Inner Child when you are experiencing emotional reaction or 'childish' resistance. As adults we may still employ forms of reactive behaviour, such as temper tantrums or moodiness, in order to get attention. Alternatively, if we are being forced to do something which truly goes against our grain, we may rebel with fighting and screaming, if sometimes inwardly, where it really hurts us.

In the next exercise you may explore how to attain a greater level of co-operation with your Inner Child by entering into a dialogue.

Learning How to Love your Inner Child

This dialogue is between you, consciously choosing the agreements and direction to the best of your ability, and your Inner Child, whose resources of energy, intuition and creative spontaneity are available to you.

Place your hands over your stomach area and extend the warmth of your loving touch into that part of your body where the Inner Child resides. If you have not yet satisfactorily made contact with your Inner Child, you might like to begin with a simple writing exercise.

With your usual writing hand, write a note to your Inner Child, beginning:

Dear Little [*Your Name*]
I want you to know how much I love and care for you. I would like us to work together better in the future. Is there anything you can tell me that will assist me to do this?
　　　　　　　　Signed:
　　　　　　　　[*Your Name*]

Writing with your non-dominant hand (i.e. the left hand if you are right-handed) enables you to express your more intuitive faculties. Now, again using that hand, write a reply from your Inner Child beginning:

Dear [*Your Name*]

and allow your Child to tell briefly whatever he or she would like. The reply does not have to be long. The important purpose here is to make the contact. As your Inner Child writes to you, notice any feelings you have. If you experience any emotions, just observe them. The reply from your Inner Child could look something like the example in Figure 3.

You might like to reflect on any requests that your Child makes to you and consider how you can incorporate them into your life. You can enjoy discovering how to bring about a greater balance of nurturing, discipline and fun within yourself **(I)**, and find that balance enhancing your relationships with others **(O)**.

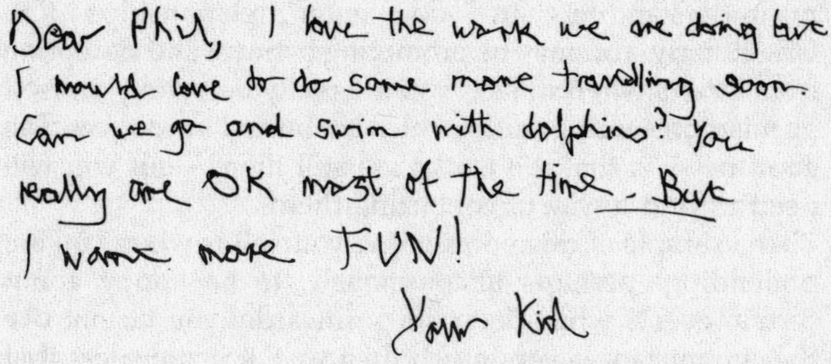

Dear Phil, I love the work we are doing but I would love to do some more travelling soon. Can we go and swim with dolphins? You really are OK most of the time. But I want more FUN!

Your Kid

Figure 3: Letter from the Inner Child.

Keep in mind the *Triangle of Trust* the next time you find yourself feeling emotionally out of balance. There is a good chance that if you first listen inwardly, you will find that you can regain inner harmony by giving attention to one or more sides of the Triangle.

The Higher Perspective

As you awaken, nurture and strengthen the relationship with your Inner Child, you may begin to realize how wonderful and remarkable the Child within you is, as indeed all children are. As adults, we may underestimate the extraordinary resources in the children around us and assume that because they are inexperienced in the ways of the world that they should be told what to do, rather than fully listened to. If, as you were growing up, the adults around you did not listen to you very much, you may not have learnt how to listen to your Inner Child. Now as an adult, you may experience a new world within you as you attune yourself **(I)** to an aspect of your nature you had formerly rejected.

As already mentioned, one of the penalties you may be

paying for lack of inner attunement (I) is that of misunderstandings in your outer relationships (O). Unwittingly, you may be promoting betrayal and deception from others when in fact, you are really betraying yourself by misrepresenting truths which are buried inside you. The good news is that the truths are still there – but you will need to find a way of contacting them.

An example of misrepresenting yourself is when you are pretending, perhaps unconsciously, to be happy about certain events while deep down inwardly you do not like the circumstances very much. In a way, it matters less that you may be 'fooling others' (O). What matters is that you may be fooling yourself (I), and living a lie. So if you lead people, and yourself, to believe that you are perfectly fine with a set of conditions but numb, deny or reject your inner misgivings, you are promoting circumstances of upset and misunderstanding for yourself (I), and probably with the others (O) that you are misleading.

Unresolved inner conflicts may pull you down until you pay attention to them. You may have experienced times when it felt as though you were in, as it were, the sub-basement of your consciousness, devoid of any creative resources, trapped and stuck. Such difficulties come about through a lack of knowing what you can do, and therefore not being able to take any action.

You might like to imagine that you could take yourself out of the sub-basement, if necessary in stages: to the basement, ground floor, mezzanine and then to the penthouse, where you might be able to see your difficulties in a better light and from a higher perspective. To be able to view your circumstances from a greater altitude assists in putting a problem into a larger picture in your life. To make the mental and emotional journey upwards, you might begin simply moving: physically getting active. To get from the ground floor to the mezzanine, finish something you have been meaning to do for a while. Keep going, while you maintain your sights on the highest level available to you. Keep a smile bubbling up inside as you go.

As your level of consciousness rises, you may get in touch with any number of resources in the forms of people who may wish to assist you and go with you as you go up. Here are found relationships of mutual growth and support (I) < > (O).

Before you get busy physically (O), you can prepare yourself inwardly (I) so that the actions you take will have the greatest benefit for you. The following exercise is one that will bring you into alignment with yourself and take you above and beyond your imagined limitations.

Taking a View from Above

This guided visualization you may do in stages, closing your eyes between each section as you inwardly do the work. More effective still might be to record the visualization on a cassette so that you can listen to it entirely within yourself without potentially being distracted by having to open your eyes. If you do this, allow a few seconds between each statement for your inner reflection.

The main theme you will be working with here is that of imagining using a clear white light, rather like air, filling a balloon so that as the balloon fills, it rises upwards. As you breathe in air, you too will be filling yourself with a crystal clear quality of light that lifts you upwards. This light is one by which you can both see and be seen, one which awakens you to your innate understanding and peaceful centre, your inner resourcefulness.

Allow yourself to become very relaxed. Sit or recline in such a way that your body is free of any pressure. Loosen tight clothing, uncross your arms and legs.

Close your eyes and locate an area in the centre of your chest where you experience warmth and loving. Take a few moments just to be with that feeling . . . Observe your breathing . . . Is your breath shallow . . . or deep . . .? Fast . . . or slow . . .?

Now take in a deep breath . . . and imagine the air entering your body through the loving centre in your chest . . . As the air enters . . . see it as a clear beam of light . . . and bring it up to the top of your head . . . As you breathe out . . . envisage the air . . . and the light extending down to your feet . . . This time breathe in deeply as before, through the centre of your chest . . . and envisage the air extending up above your head a few inches before breathing out . . . and, as you breathe out, envisage the air, the light, extending down to your feet . . . and beyond . . . Push the air out of your lungs so that they are as empty as you can make them . . .

Repeat this breathing exercise a couple of times . . .

Now, whatever the obstacle was that you encountered, see it as a dot, somewhere below you, very indistinct . . . As you do the breathing exercise, envisage yourself becoming lighter and lighter . . . lifting above any concerns . . . into a state of calm and peacefulness . . . a world of perfect relaxation and inner attunement . . .

See yourself now on the highest floor of a tall, tall building . . . You can see for miles around . . . all kinds of scenery – rivers . . . hills . . . valleys . . . tiny houses . . . factories . . . lakes . . . forests . . . It is awe-inspiring . . . There is a beauty that is impossible for you to define . . . Spend a few moments now just enjoying that magnificent beauty all around you . . .

At this great altitude, you also feel completely safe . . . You feel a sense of joy and inner freedom like never before . . . Anything is possible . . . you have no limitations . . . In this location of safety and calm, you are now in touch with your inmost sense of who you are . . . radiant, resourceful and clear . . .

Maintaining those qualities within you, imagine yourself descending through the building . . . floor by floor . . . quite rapidly . . . until you come to the mezzanine . . . Stop there for a few moments and look out and around your immediate environment . . . You may notice just below you the next actions you have to take . . . Allow yourself to come very gently once again down to the ground floor . . . keeping the clear, radiant and resourceful qualities within you . . .

Move your hands and feet . . . become aware more consciously of your surroundings . . . take in a deep breath and stretch . . .

Make any notes that you would like to about your experience. You might like to list some of the possible next actions you will take. Agree to yourself a time by which you will have completed the first one.

Understanding – An Intuitive Response

Most of us have been well-educated in reasoning and the kind of understanding that comes from directly applying our minds to getting us from A to B. Our minds are a great resource when handling knowable facts. What should be considered is that the mind has gathered 'facts' from past experiences which need not have any relevance to present or future conditions. We live in a world where change is the order of the day.

In the area of our relationships we constantly encounter the unknown in ourselves (I) and others (O). In such cases, understanding may bear no relation to anything our mind could have reasoned, but can come intuitively, through the contact between Inspirational Self and Inner Child.

It may not be until you feel stuck that you actively seek understanding as a way out. You may try hard to work out the reasons why you got there in the first place and what you can do about it now, without really knowing clearly the outcome you would like to have. This mental activity can produce emotional tension and close the door to your source of inner awareness.

A valuable alternative is to admit to yourself:

♥ 'I don't know how . . .'
♥ 'I don't know what . . .'
♥ 'I don't know why . . .'
♥ 'I don't know where . . .'

'I don't know . . .' is like opening a door to your deeper resources of wisdom and understanding.

Act or React – The Choice is Yours

It takes great strength sometimes to admit, firstly to yourself **(I)** and then to those whose approval you care to have **(O)**, that you are vulnerable and that their words and actions can hurt you. The closer someone is to us, the greater the risk of potential loss of approval. Fear, this time of possibly losing a person whose loving we value, obscures our capacity for honouring our inner alignment or integrity.

The following exercise is designed to assist you to reach inwardly for your own sources of guidance, assistance and wisdom so that you can, with this attunement, consciously translate *Inspiration* into *Action*. This works best with as open and positive a frame of mind as possible in order to *redirect* the negative emotion, such as self-doubt, fear, anxiety, anger, etc., to produce a greater experience of happiness and contentment within you.

Know that within you, you have access to the most remarkable wealth of information that can supply all your needs. Gaining access to this reservoir of understanding is a matter of knowing:

a. which question(s) to ask
b. how to ask them (with an open mind and positively)

Other factors that are important to bear in mind are:

a. answers will come to you, although not necessarily instantly

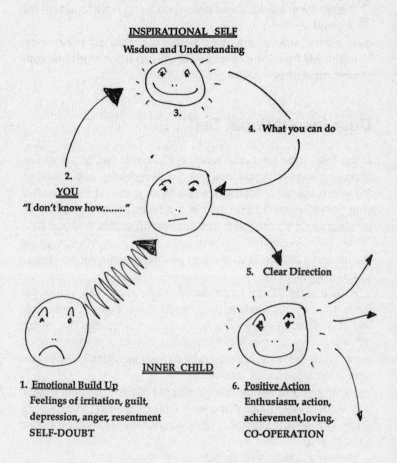

INSPIRATIONAL SELF

Wisdom and Understanding

3.

4. What you can do

2.
YOU
"I don't know how........"

5. Clear Direction

INNER CHILD

1. Emotional Build Up
   Feelings of irritation, guilt,
   depression, anger, resentment
   SELF-DOUBT

6. Positive Action
   Enthusiasm, action,
   achievement, loving,
   CO-OPERATION

Figure 4: Inspiration to Action

b. so remember to be patient
c. you may need to address your mind to an issue underlying the one you asked about before knowing how to act on the original
d. answers may come directly from within or may come indirectly from one or more others, so listen both inwardly and outwardly

Dear Inspirational Self . . .

In the heat of an emotional reaction **(I)**, it may not be the easiest thing to step to one side, in a manner of speaking, and reflect on the wisest course of action. It would be an excellent investment of your time therefore to stop, take in a deep breath and count to ten before striking yourself with self-criticism **(I)** or out in anger **(O)**.

This exercise assumes that there is a solution available to you in the form of a clear way forward, so you must keep your mind open to this possibility.

Write a letter to your Inspirational Self (you can give him or her a name if you would like) and read it through last thing at night before you go to sleep. Sometimes it is not until we sleep that we 'switch off' our conscious minds sufficiently for our inner worlds to go to work on our behalf. It is particularly difficult to switch off when we have a testing issue to resolve.

The letter is best written with a note of positive expectancy about it. You could even imagine you were writing on behalf of your Inner Child. The following morning, your Inspirational Self will be writing back to you.

The letters could look something like these:

Dear Jack **(IS)**,
I am having a hard time caring for Bob at the moment. He is always letting me down. When he says we are going to do something, we end up not doing it and I feel disappointed. I am so fed up I do not really want to bother seeing him. I would

like some ideas about how I can talk to him about it, without feeling angry with him and telling him to get lost. I want to feel again the loving I have for him.

Love from Sue

Dear Sue,
Thank you for remembering to ask me. I had been feeling rather redundant up here. Is Bob having a hard time loving himself at the moment? If he is, it might be hard for you to feel the loving you have for him. It might be better not to expect anything of him for a while. Best not to hold his behaviour against you. Why don't you relax and do something really loving for yourself today and give Bob some space?
   I love you very much.

Jack

Your letters could look very different from these so allow yourself to write spontaneously and freely whatever comes to mind. You may be amazed by the responses you receive. If the issue, or upset, is a very complex one, you may need to repeat this exercise more than once until you have the awareness you seek.

The Power of Positive Digestion

We are inevitably subject to negativity, whether it is on a local and personal level, such as in the pain of our loved ones, or on a more general level, as in news items of human devastation from around the world. It may be out of your empathy with a friend in need who has expressed his grief (O), or the hate directed towards you by an adversary. The fact is that if you feel the hurt inside you (I), that is where it was in the first place. Outer circumstances or events simply made you aware of an existing condition within yourself. If you take on too much more from the outside you will find yourself on emotional overload and the 'toxic burden' may become indigestible. It is important that we accept our vulnerability and that we carry areas of pain within us. In learning to love and take better care of ourselves **(I)**, we can choose to be with the people and circumstances that more fully allow and promote our inner healing.

Whatever its origin, the negativity in our lives offers us an opportunity for enrichment. You do not have to return anger and hurt with yet more hurt and anger. It is sometimes necessary to stand back in order to digest the negative build-up within you. Then you need to discard what is toxic to your system by letting go of that over which you have no control. Finally, turn the raw energy, in the light of your compassion, into some positive and constructive use.

This principle is perhaps best illustrated by the waste recycling worms who are 'employed' in eating all kinds of decaying rubbish (food for them), together with abrasive sand, to produce valuable loam for market gardening in areas where soil is at a premium. Similarly, with the power of positive digestion, we can derive raw energy from any sources of negativity and translate it into something enriching for ourselves and others. The pain in ourselves and the world often defies any sensible explanation. Yet it has been said that enough loving heals all things.

It is our considerable resources of loving that form the digestive juices at our disposal. Those resources are not only within us, but within every other person and are to be found in the usually silent presence of our Inspirational Self.

You may be aware of the concept that in order to be understood, you must first learn understanding. The power of positive digestion is our choice of caring and compassion. When we witness scenes of violence we may react **(I)** by shooting our arrows of righteous indignation at the participants **(O)**. Or alternatively, we could look within ourselves to heal our own violence.

The greatest challenge to our capacity for understanding lies not with those conflicts at some distance from us but those immediately on our doorstep, with our 'neighbours'. Our neighbours here could live across a national border, belong to an opposing political party, express cultural, religious or tribal differences of belief and behaviour, or even be members of the same family.

This next exercise offers you the chance to digest, or break down, some of the bitterness and abrasion you may be holding *inside yourself* against an 'enemy'.

Caring and Compassion – Digestive Enzymes

Bring to mind the person or particular group of people who most arouses negative emotion within you. It could be a family member such as a step-father or daughter-in-law; a Protestant, if you are a Catholic in Ireland; blacks if you are white in Georgia; Jews, if you are an Arab in Israel; a teacher if you are a student; a devotee if you are a guru; a warder if you are a prisoner.

Now switch on your caring and compassion. List 20 positive qualities you can perceive and appreciate in your 'enemy'. This does not mean you have to like the individual or group, but simply look at the good they have going for them. For example, even during the World Wars, the British and German soldiers had an appreciation of and read each other's literature – and even respected their battle techniques. English soldiers enjoyed listening to Brahms and Beethoven.

If you can focus your mind on the good aspects of people that you thought you hated, this digestive process of concentration on the goodness gradually dissolves the hate, because it is difficult to hate someone you appreciate.

So, with this exercise, you can break down, or digest, whatever has been poisoning *your* system. It may make no difference whatsoever to the object **(O)** of your former bitterness. You are the one who will derive the nourishment of your own **(I)** caring and compassion.

A Final Reminder

In the best acts of loving, there is not really one person who gives and another who receives, because there is only one action truly taking place. What we are striving for **(I)** are those moments of being at *one* with those others **(O)** with whom we are in relationship. That is a consciousness of understanding.

Chapter 3

Peace

. . . Becoming a Friend to Yourself (I) and Others (O)

If you were to look around you, you might think that we were not really designed for peace. Drama and conflict seem to thrive on every street corner. Television, radio and general conversation often abound with differences of opinion, clashes of temperament and fighting. Given then our nature, we have plenty of excuse to treat life as a battle – that's certainly the way it looks sometimes!

In fact, the journey towards the discovery of a peaceful co-existence with others **(O)** will prove to be more challenging, exciting and ultimately rewarding than a hands-on fisticuffs approach to life. You may still be doing battle in a sense, but the main opposition will be your own internal forces of conflict **(I)**. So you see, peace is far from dull. Also, in terms of conquering your inner worlds of personal doubt, misgiving, fear, anger or stress, it is unlikely that you will stake your claim for 'peace' as a 'one time and forever' mission. Generally speaking, the enemy within keeps us on our toes. It seems to have profound communication with those around us, usually those closest to us, who serve to point up our next field of endeavour on the peace front. So there is always progress to be made . . .

What exactly is peace, anyway? It has been said that it is the absence of conflict. But there is a much more positive stand that we can take to produce the experience of peace within us. Explore with the following exercise your own meaning of peace. You may find you get some really interesting insights and discover a deeper sense of your personal values and motivation.

What is Peace for Me?

The first part of this exercise is to draw one simple symbol that represents what peace means for you. It could be a 'nonsensical' shape something like a doodle. Or it could represent a specific object like a tree, a television, a dolphin or a house. Take a piece of paper and spontaneously draw whatever comes to mind (Figure 5 is an example).

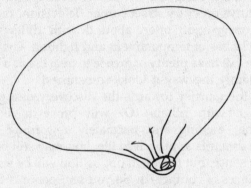

Figure 5: My symbol of peace.

Write one or more sentences describing how your drawing represents peace to you.

For example:

I have drawn a rose petal – it would be pink if I could colour it, and it has a delicate scent. It represents peace to me because it is very soft to touch and it gives of itself in a gentle, non-demanding way. It is also complete in itself, although it is part of a whole flower, and alone is very beautiful.

Then complete the following statement at least ten times:

   Peace is . . .

Allow your thoughts to flow freely without censorship. Even if what comes to mind seems strange, carry on with the exercise. The very next thought may the one that strikes a chord for you.
   For example:

♥ Peace is productivity.
♥ Peace is humming.
♥ Peace is effortless breath.
♥ Peace is vibrancy.
♥ Peace is spontaneity.
♥ Peace is in the moment now.
♥ Peace is attaining inner peace.
♥ Peace is a state of personal resourcefulness.
♥ Peace is loving.
♥ Peace is the release from conflict.
♥ Peace is gaps between activity.
♥ Peace is being actively, enthusiastically involved in life.
♥ Peace is a deeper level of acceptance.
♥ Peace is receiving.
♥ Peace is vulnerable.
♥ Peace is now.

This is an important exercise to do to begin to identify your own experience of peace. Your own experience may have little to do with what you may have been told, or have believed, in the past.

Cultivate Positive Peace

The more you sow and cultivate seeds of positivity within, the more you are nurturing your inner world of happiness. With a positive orientation, you will see the positive purpose behind all conflicts, disturbances and disagreements. As you turn any inner condition of negativity **(I)** into one of peacefulness, you may also become adept at doing the same towards those around you **(O)**. Take, for example, other people's 'bad' habits which affect your own well-being – habits such as meanness, laziness, aggression, untidiness, lateness for appointments, dishonesty, thoughtlessness, manipulation . . . you can probably add a few more. Feeling critical and self-righteous does nothing either to change anyone else's behaviour or to further good feelings within yourself. You might choose to enter into battle, either actively by arguing or passively by withholding your loving. But another possibility is to recognize that such people are bringing you a gift.

The gift in this case is perhaps like a model aircraft kit. You need to put it together, assemble it, get involved with it until it takes the form of the picture on the outside of the box. In its dismantled form, you might not be able to imagine the gift completed. You may need a little time and space to put it together, perhaps some leisure time when you are relaxed and unstressed.

This next exercise is one in which you will be nurturing greater alignment between your Inner Child and Inspirational Self. Drawing upon the resources of your Inspirational Self, you will be receiving guidance through your creative imagination.

Recognizing the Gifts in Camouflaged Wrapping

Take in a few deep breaths and allow yourself to become quiet inside. Imagine a warm sun shining down on you, even if you are indoors and it is cold and raining outside. Place your hands over your stomach and make contact with your Inner Child. Allow the warmth from your hands to ease any tightness or tension you may be holding in that area of your body. Reassuring the Child within you of your love will assist you to relax and open to your sources of inner guidance.

You will need a pen and paper for the dialogue part of this exercise. First of all, bring to mind someone who causes you to feel frustration, irritation, depression, anger or any other form of personal stress. Reflect on the following questions.

♥ What is the behaviour or attitude that you find particularly disturbing or upsetting?
♥ What is the gift they are bringing to you?
  (It is fine to admit for now 'I don't know' – remember this statement can be a first step to opening a door to your awareness, if you keep yourself open to receive it.)
♥ Is it an opportunity to be of service to them in some way, receiving through giving to them?
♥ Is it a chance to practise honesty, courage, tolerance or patience and develop a personal strength?
♥ How can you be creative inside yourself in relation to this person?
♥ Is the person giving you an insight into some aspect of your own attitude or behaviour which you would now like to improve?
♥ What is the personal quality that you can now enhance in order to have a peaceful relationship with him/her inside yourself?
♥ How can you best receive the gift that this person is bringing to you?

You might like to appreciate the co-operation of your Inner Child for assisting you to become more aware of some of the issues in this relationship which has been challenging to you as the adult, who has now seen more clearly into the nature of the personal resources of wisdom.

This part of the exercise is to be done in the form of a dialogue with your Inspirational Self **(IS)**. A role of your Inspirational Self is to assist and guide you towards and through those relationship experiences which can serve you, in ways that are most nurturing and uplifting. Using any of the questions above, or other questions that might come to mind, remember that you are looking for the gift, the blessing in disguise, and are open to receive it. To give you an idea, here is an example.

Me: The person that I find especially irritating is Freddy. He has a sneery attitude – I always feel he is out to make fun of me and poke his nose into my affairs. On top of which he is too clever by half, but he hasn't got his own act together at all. He is a real pain.

IS: It sounds as though he may have done something to hurt you.

Me: The weird thing is that he has not done anything I can really put my finger on. When he is in any kind of proximity to me, it feels as though he is looking for reasons to put me down or to ridicule me in some way. It is as though he is looking for something really distasteful about me that he can elaborate on to tell other people. You know how a person talks to someone else behind their hand while looking at you?

IS: I can understand how that must be very uncomfortable for you, emotionally hurtful. Is that so?

Me: Well, yes. I do not usually feel at ease in his presence and I try to avoid him at all costs.

IS: Would you be willing to explore and discover the blessing in disguise in this relationship?

Me: OK. I have absolutely no idea what that could be.

IS: Fine. Can you think what it could be in Freddy's behaviour that you might not like in yourself?

Me: I think it is that for some reason, he resents me.

IS: Do you mean that he would like you to be something that you are not?

Me: I am not 100 per cent sure, but that's what it seems like to me.

IS: So if Freddy were a mirror to you, you could have a negatively critical attitude towards yourself. You might

be wanting yourself to be something that you are not.
Is that possible?

Me: That is possible. But what can I do about that?

IS: It will be difficult to do anything so long as you are
reacting towards Freddy with irritation. The first step
is to *observe* your feelings of irritation, instead of
projecting them onto Freddy. Observation will take some
of the heat out of them.

Me: A bit like putting soothing ointment on a bee sting?

IS: That sort of thing.

Me: Then what?

IS: To use the bee analogy, the next time you feel irritated,
watch where you 'put' yourself, your 'emotions', that
make you vulnerable to being 'stung'. In a sense, you
have been setting yourself up to feel irritated.

Me: I don't really see how.

IS: Perhaps that is the purpose of having this experience
with Freddy. He is showing you, enabling you to see
how you do that. Only you have to observe yourself
inwardly to find out that information.

Me: OK. So I find out what I do to set myself up to be
irritated. Then what?

IS: Once you accept that bees do indeed sting, that Freddy
has a capacity for irritating you, you can take care of
yourself when you are with Freddy so that you do not
have to get irritated. After all, knowing that a bee
stings, you would not go out of your way to get stung.
You respect that stinging is part of its nature and that
your skin is sensitive.

Me: Is there anything more you can tell me?

IS: You are going to have to practise doing the observation
a few times before I can really give you any further
suggestions.

Me: OK. Thank you. That is really helpful. So one of the
gifts that Freddy is bringing me is teaching me to
respect my sensitivity and take better care of myself

	when I am in the presence of 'bees'.
IS:	Sounds good to me. Well done! I love you.
Me:	I love you too.

Allow yourself to be very spontaneous once again – the best way of ensuring a response from your inner resources – and use the questions as a guideline as you go about discovering the gift being brought to you. Have as much fun as possible. This will assist you to distance yourself from any disturbance you may have been experiencing.

Finally, acknowledge and appreciate your Inner Child for being willing to co-operate with you in doing this exercise. Be aware that you may receive further insights in the course of your day while walking, showering or mowing the lawn!

Receiving your Peace

In the example of the last exercise was a significant clue to discovering your internal peace in personal relationships. It was that if you receive and feel good enough about yourself, you *can* receive what you most want deep down. If you have all kinds of barriers within you, such as an overly critical attitude towards yourself, blocking your capacity for receiving, you will neither accept the gifts that others bring to you **(O)**, nor will you receive fully the qualities inherent within you **(I)**.

The Peace Cycle

The *Peace Cycle* below illustrates a process of producing internal peace in relationship with others. You will recognize the themes from the previous chapters being integrated with the objective of peace in view.

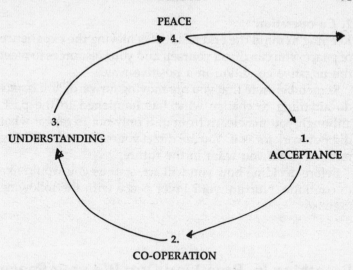

Figure 6: The Peace Cycle.

1. Acceptance

Whether the obstacle you encounter in a relationship is within you or outside you, you need to accept its presence. This could be the behaviour, action or attitude of someone with whom you live or work, for example, or it could be an emotional reaction you experience under certain circumstances. Start the Peace Cycle by observing and making a statement of acceptance like one of the following:

♥ I accept that I feel guilty for hitting out at Shirley.

♥ I accept that Jim smokes cigarettes.

♥ I accept that I get irritable when Bob is hanging about doing nothing.

♥ I accept that Barbara needs a lot of support from her friends now.

♥ I accept that I value my privacy.

♥ I accept that Ed is never on time when we arrange to meet up.

2. Co-operation

Keeping in mind the end result of achieving the experience of peace, you can direct yourself and your resources to meet the negative condition in a positive way.

Remember here that you are moving forward. You *cannot* do anything to change what has happened in the past, although you may learn from it, if only not to repeat what did not work for you. You *can* direct yourself into producing more of what you want in the future.

Before deciding how you will act, start as you would like to continue. Nurture your inner peace with the following exercise:

Breathing In–Breathing Out: It's your Peace

You may choose anywhere or anytime to do this exercise. Take as long as you like. Stop whatever you are doing. You can stand or sit down.

First of all, just observe your breathing. Watch, if you can, the air as it enters your body and then leaves. Notice if your breathing is shallow or rushed.

Then, very gently and gradually, slowly breathe in more deeply and exhale more fully, all the time observing the passage of the air.

Next, breathe to steady counts of five as follows:

♥ Breathe in (to the count of five).
♥ Hold your breath (to the count of five).
♥ Exhale (to the count of five).
♥ Stay exhaled (to the count of five).
♥ Breathe in again.
♥ Hold your breath. Etc.

Do this a few times until you feel calmer and more at peace with yourself, until you have restored your inner equilibrium.

Now review your creative options for addressing the relationship challenge you identified. You might like to reflect on the following questions:

♥ What did you learn from past actions or behaviour?
♥ What can you do right now – **(I)** or **(O)**?
♥ What can you do differently in the future?

For example:

♥ I learnt that Ed is reliably late for his appointments.
♥ I can do nothing to change Ed. Saying something to him in the past never made any difference.
♥ I can allow an extra 15 minutes when we arrange to meet so that our 'timing' coincides. Or, if it is important, I do not have to wait and can go without him.

or

♥ I learnt that I love Shirley too much to want to strike out at her.
♥ I can stay in touch with the loving feelings I have for her.
♥ I can ask her to clear up her room when she gets home.

or

♥ I learnt that my values differ from Bob's.
♥ I can feel grateful that he is not hanging around me right now.
♥ Instead of projecting my set of values onto Bob and getting bad-tempered I can concentrate on doing what is important for me.

3. Understanding
Name at least one gift of understanding you have received that contributes towards your experience of peace. This is the point at which you are integrating your challenges to gain greater attunement within yourself **(I)** and with those

who were instrumental in your learning **(O)**. You may recall that the consciousness of understanding is one in which you discard the differences and realize what you have in common.

For example:

♥ The gift of understanding I received from Ed is my capacity to be flexible and to be true to myself.
♥ The gift of understanding I received from Shirley was that I love her much more than I care about how she leaves her room.
♥ The gift of understanding I received from Bob is that there is room in the world for his approach to life and mine.

4. Peace

Once you have fully opened yourself to receive the gifts being brought to you, you are likely to experience a new quality of fullness or plenty, the quality that accompanies peace. The plenty may show up in the form of enthusiasm, a sense of fun, increased vitality or even the feeling of gratitude for your life.

Each gift of learning **(I)**, however apparently small, can have a tremendous positive impact on your future relationships **(O)**. Award yourself a Peace Graduation Award as an acknowledgment of your progress thus far. The award does not have to be large but it is better if it is tangible, a small gift to yourself that's probably best not shown to others.

One suggestion you might like to follow is to write yourself an award and ask a friend to mail it to you in two weeks' time. You may find that it arrives just in time to remind you how you addressed a challenge positively and that if you did it once, you can do it again.

For example:

PEACE GRADUATION AWARD

Congratulations!
[Your Name]
You met the challenge of _____
presented to you by _____
and received the following gift of
understanding _____
_____
_____

I love you

Riding the Rough Terrain

You may experience times when riding the Peace Cycle is
easy going, like coasting down a smooth gentle hill with
rolling green countryside all around you, a warm sun and
a fresh breeze contributing to your pleasure and
enjoyment. At other times the road seems pot-holed and
strewn with rocks that throw you off balance, and
emotional storms lash around you. Yet it is often when you
are most challenged that your greatest gifts are being
brought to you.

In relationships, both with yourself and others, you may
well have unknowingly developed habits that make the
going rough for you **(I)**. Such habitual patterns, that were
perhaps once important for your sense of survival, could
include hiding behind clever remarks, using humour to
distract others from your vulnerability, keeping your
distance from others by being 'all-knowing', aggressively
demanding that others do things your way or avoiding

intimacy through promiscuity. The good news is that if *you* **(I)** put the rocks and pot-holes on the road, you can also take them away. The bad news is that you might have criticized or judged yourself harshly for having caused the difficulty initially – in which case, you will find it hard to even see the obstacles, far less remove them to receive your peace!

The barrier to awareness could be envisaged as a barricade. Like any fortification, it was once erected for your protection and served a purpose for you (remember the 'rock wall' in the last chapter). But as you learn and grow strengths through your life experiences, your barricades may become redundant and need to be dismantled because they take your precious energy to be maintained. They may also contain old hurts arising from ancient misunderstandings. Now could be a good time to let them all go and move on, free of them.

Dismantling your Barricades

Although for this exercise you will be dismantling your barricade, know you can rebuild it for as long as you need it. For now, in the safety and security of your own inner world, you are simply experimenting by stepping beyond its bounds and feeling what it might be like on the outside, just creating a new set of choices for yourself. Subsequently, you might like to step outside from time to time, have the experience of freedom, then return to the old protection. Gradually, like a bird spreading its wings, you may learn to fly free from the former limiting conditions. But only when you are ready to do so.

This is a drawing exercise. The first part is to draw your barricade. It could be wood, stone, logs, a reinforced concrete structure, whatever represents most accurately the protection you have given to yourself against the world. Put in as much detail as you would like. Your barrier can be very solid, but allow one tiny peephole in the structure so that you can just see out. As far as possible, draw your barricade intuitively, without thinking too hard about it. Figure 7 is an example.

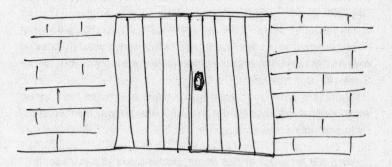

Figure 7: My barricade.

In a few words, describe what you have drawn. For example:

Heavy wooden castle door. Stone walls on either side of it.

Simply observing your barricade may tell you much about the nature of your protection.

The next part of the exercise involves dismantling it.

The barricade went up probably for some very good reason. You may feel hesitant about even looking beyond it, far less removing it. However, in the time since you first erected it, you will have grown and developed many skills and understanding. In that time, you can imagine that that from which you once protected yourself has transformed. Now, if you look through the gap in your barricade, you can glimpse a scene of great peace and beauty. It could be a view of nature, of harmonious relationships in your home or any other outlook that is nurturing for you.

Here you can invite your Inner Child to be as creative as he/she wishes in dismantling the barricade. Anything from earth-moving equipment to a magic wand may be employed for this task. A special gift awaits your Child on the other side of the barricade.

Close your eyes for a few moments and allow your Child to have fun dismantling the barricade and to discover that what is on the other side is even greater than the glimpse they saw before. The gift is very obvious. Let the Child take and hold it. What is the gift? What does it feel like? What does it look like? Is there any sound associated with your gift? What previously hidden positive aspect of your nature is now in your hands?

When you open your eyes again, make any notes about your experience of dismantling the wall and the gift you claimed.

For example:

> *My Child felt stuck at first about dismantling the barricade. It looked too powerful and immovable. But on looking through the gap she got excited. She tried pushing with her shoulder at first but that did not work. Then she invited some super-powerful chemical solvent to be poured over the barricade. As the solvent dissolved and evaporated, the barricade disappeared with it. No trace was left behind. Stepping over where the barricade had once been felt a little scary. But there were lots of green fields in sunshine. Her gift was a tiny bird, very soft; she could feel its heart beating in her hands, she could hear a faint sound from its beak. Its feathers were gold and blue. The qualities represented by the bird were sensitivity and the freedom to enjoy the scene, and to fly from danger when necessary.*

This exercise will give you certain insights about yourself and the nature of your own peace. When you have completed it, be aware of these insights as they reflect in your everyday life. And be gentle with yourself. Rome itself was neither built, nor dismantled, in a day.

Peace, Perfect Peace

Our ideals of peace seldom coincide with reality. Our ideal might be one of unfettered personal pleasure **(I)**, with the rest of the world **(O)** conforming to that picture. From day one, a baby human is deciding: 'This experience gives me pleasure and therefore must be good (and right)' and 'That experience gives me pain and therefore must be bad (and wrong).' Judging certain aspects of experience, of non-conforming, sometimes pain-inflicting others **(O)**, or their actions as being bad or wrong is a way of distancing ourselves **(I)** from them. In this sense of the word, judgement has a negative emotional response with it, a shutting down of our capacity for loving acceptance.

In addition to discovering how others do not measure up to our ideal images, we may find *ourselves* falling short of the approval of some imaginary quality controller, or judge, out there determining whether we are worthwhile or scheduled for the scrap heap. So not only do we judge and resent others **(O)**, but we also judge ourselves and then find ourselves **(I)** feeling guilty.

The terrible twins of Guilt and Resentment create a negative force field within us that separates us from our sources and experience of loving. They often go hand in hand and are perhaps the greatest factor contributing to our lack of ease, or peace, within ourselves.

Yet always remember that through a combination of compassion, kindness and self-awareness we can learn new habits to replace hurt feelings with happiness. If a thought, word or action you took yesterday was non-productive, you do not need to repeat it today.

Exploring Guilt and Resentment

There is nothing you can do today to change an action you took a year back, yesterday or even five minutes ago. Those

actions are part of your unchangeable history: simply facts.
If you said something inadvertently that hurt your mother
last week, that moment has long since past. You may
nevertheless carry a residual feeling of *guilt* about it. On top
of that, you may resent your mother for having 'caused' you
to be hurtful. As a result, you may find yourself caught in
the *Guilt/Resentment Trap*. The way this works is that pieces
of history with guilt or resentment attached may get buried
(I), and only revealed years later in your subsequent
relationships with others **(O)**. There *is*, however, an
important trap door which can positively trigger your
release. More about that later.

However intelligent and wise we are, we can never really
see the full picture of our own, or anyone else's, life. When
we are judgemental towards ourselves and produce feelings
of guilt **(I)**, or towards others and produce feelings of
resentment **(O)**, we are assuming that *we* always know
'right' from 'wrong', 'good' from 'bad'. In reality, however,
certain circumstances are not clearly white and black. There
are many shades of grey.

When we need to demonstrate that we are 'right'
(implying that others are 'wrong'), it can often be because
we feel insecure, because deep down there is a worm of
self-doubt gnawing away inside us. When you can love the
worm, by accepting that you do not have the full picture
of your own or anyone else's life, you can *use* your emotions
of guilt and resentment as sources of information.

By becoming aware of *how* your judgements – **(I)** *and*
(O) – limit your experience of loving, you can gain freedom
from the pattern of perpetual hurting. In order to do this,
you may need to revise your ideal images concerning
yourself **(I)** and others **(O)** to achieve greater happiness.

Consider the following, which might be as true for you
(I) as for all those with whom you come into contact **(O)**:

What if, at all times,
we are doing the best we can
with what we know;
if we knew better,
then we might do better.

The following exercise is important for becoming aware of your self-image, and the ways you may be 'violating' it. When you become aware of the limited opinions, negative thoughts or judgements you are holding *against* yourself, you can extend greater caring and compassion *towards* yourself. The more ease you can attain within yourself **(I)**, the more you will feel at ease with others **(O)**.

What will be valuable here is to see and accept yourself beyond a set of beliefs, self-image and perhaps some arbitrary standards of perfection (*see* Chapter 1); to recognize that you have inwardly chosen possibly unreasonable and harsh rules for yourself. You may now negotiate a more compassionate set of boundaries, including a kinder, more accepting self-image, within which you can live with greater personal freedom and happiness.

Liberation from Guilt and Resentment

Guilt and resentment are part of being human and, even though they are emotionally negative, nevertheless do serve a purpose. If you have consciously set yourself on a certain course, the pinprick of guilt, if you are aware of it, will let you know when you are off track. You may, for example, resolve to be more patient, tender and caring with your spouse but feel guilty when you lose your temper again, having broken a commitment you made.

From time to time, however, the emotions of guilt and resentment may become overwhelming and make you judge yourself as a 'bad' person. If you can stand back, *observe* and *learn from them, you are a step towards redirecting the energy they block, and deriving greater fulfilment in your relationships with yourself* **(I)** *and others* **(O)**.

The two emotions are explored together here because, as mentioned above, they are often interlinked. To take another example, you may resent your sister for losing your sweater and then feel guilty about not being loving towards her.

First of all, let's look at guilt. Take a pen and paper and write down the answers to the following questions:

1. Recall a time you felt guilty, past or present.
2. What did you do?
3. What belief or self-image did that action violate?
4. How can you now accept yourself more fully?
   i.e. change the action, if that is possible *or*
   change the belief about your self-image *and*
   acknowledge that you are a good person who sometimes does not-so-good things.

For example:

1. I was doing some voluntary work at a friend's office.
2. I stole some stationery items from the store room.
3. As a volunteer, I should be giving to the organization and not taking from it. A good person gives and does not take.
4. At the time, I was too shy to ask for something I needed and could have offered to pay for. It is too long ago to change the action. I can accept myself more fully by acknowledging that I am a good person, who is giving, and sometimes I am reluctant to ask for what I want.

Next, similarly explore resentment with a pen and paper, answering the following questions:

1. Recall a time you felt resentment, past or present.
2. Whom did you resent?

3. What belief or rule did that person violate?
4. How can you change your belief and become more accepting of yourself and others?

> i.e. you are not in a position to change others' behaviour your *choice* is one of changing your attitude **(I)** towards them and changing your belief **(I)** about the way they are you may in turn experience greater freedom towards yourself **(I)**.

For example:

1. The time was when I was studying for exams.
2. I resented my teachers for telling me that I had to go to university after leaving school.
3. They violated the belief I held that my teachers (or other people) know what is best for me. What I knew for myself was that I did not want to go to university.
4. I can change the belief about others knowing what I want for myself. I can accept that I am the one who must decide what I want for myself and accept that my teachers were advising me to the best of their knowledge and ability.

To complete this exercise, suspend your analytical and critical functions temporarily and write statements beginning:

> *'I accept that I am a good person who sometimes . . .'*

or

> *'I accept that —— is a good person who sometimes . . .'*
> (Admit it, no one consistently does the same 'bad thing' *all the time . . .)*

Complete the statements with insights you received from the first parts of the exercise or with any response that occurs spontaneously as you are writing. See if you can let your pen do the thinking.

For example:

- ♥ I accept that I am a good person who is sometimes dishonest.
- ♥ I accept that my teachers were good people who did not always give me the best advice.

The emotions of guilt and resentment can poison your system, if you allow old issues to remain unresolved, and take you on a downward spiral unless you take action to stop yourself. But it *is* within your power to arrest the judgements when they occur, learn from all of your experiences and become more accepting of yourself **(I)** and others **(O)**.

Forget – or Regret

When we are separated inwardly from our loving **(I)**, we are separated outwardly **(O)** from those who love and care for us and wish us well. We block our own channels from *receiving* and feel isolated or lonely. This is because it is our capacity for receiving **(I)** that allows us to give to others **(O)** unconditionally and joyfully.

In order to reconnect with our own loving we must first forgive ourselves for past actions. By looking back over the past we can evaluate the results of our actions – and were we truly to assess the *value* of past experience with an attitude of positive appreciation, we would receive the benefits of personal enrichment. Our mistakes make fertile ground for future fulfilment.

Forgiving **(I)** releases us from the separation of our negative emotions and enables us to come into increased inner alignment. Whether we forgive ourselves, or someone else, we are the primary beneficiary. When we have truly forgiven, the hurts will be erased from our memory and forgotten. The forgiving heart is one that heals old hurts and frees your capacity to experience **(I)** and express **(O)** unconditional loving.

Forgiving Yourself (I)

Before you can forgive anyone else **(O)**, you need to forgive yourself for whatever you may have been holding against yourself **(I)**. Negativity drives a wedge between your Inner Child **(IC)** and Inspirational Self **(IS)**. This exercise is one in which you can reunite the two with forgiveness.

Allow yourself to be very relaxed and open so that you can *receive* the maximum benefit from the exercise. Your Inner Child will be having an opportunity to make contact and say whatever he/she wants to your Inspirational Self by means of a written dialogue.

Allow your Child to express the emotional content of your experience, to speak freely, openly and honestly without restraint. Do not attempt in any way to criticize or to prevent your feelings from being expressed. The loving of your Inspirational Self is totally accepting – the Inspirational Self has in a sense 'seen and heard it all before'. Nothing you can express will shock, upset, disturb or in any way cause your Inspirational Self to stop loving you.

Your Child may wish to talk about some unresolved issue from the past or a situation he/she is facing now which is in some way disturbing. Allow the process of forgiving to take place through the active presence of your Inspirational Self. You might imagine your Inspirational Self as being like a wise and unconditionally loving grandparent who has only your best interests at heart.

If you are not sure what subject to discuss, close your eyes for a moment, take in a deep breath, let the breath out and just notice the first thought that pops into your head. That is the one to use.

Here is an example:

IS: Good morning. How are you doing?
IC: Pretty good.
IS: Do you have something that is bothering you at the moment?

IC: Yes, as you happen to mention it.

IS: Can you tell me something about it?

IC: It's Shirley. She is so pushy and I always find that we get persuaded to do things she wants when I don't really want to do them.

IS: Is there anything else about Shirley?

IC: She always seems to be stressed and I get caught up in her problems. Not always, perhaps. But I often seem to feel anxious when she is around.

IS: Do you have to spend time with her?

IC: No. But I feel guilty because I do not feel like helping her with her problems. I feel that if I were a good person, I would make the effort to overcome the negative feelings I have about her and almost 'save her from herself'. But I don't want to.

IS: Has anyone told you that you have *got* to do anything for her.

IC: No.

IS: I am really glad you are telling me about this. Have you been giving yourself a bit of a hard time over Shirley?

IC: Yes.

IS: Do you have a sense of obligation towards her?

IC: Yes.

IS: Can you tell me something about that?

IC: When I see someone in difficulty, I feel I have to rescue them somehow.

IS: Even if it is not the best thing to do?

IC: If someone wants me to help them, I have to do *something*, don't I?

IS: Who says?

IC: Good people do things for others.

IS: Even when 'they' are emotionally 'unequipped' to do so?

IC: What do you mean?

IS: It may be difficult to be loving and giving towards a person who disturbs you.

IC: How can I be more loving towards her?

IS: Tell me first of all how you can be more loving towards yourself?

IC: I don't know.

IS: Could you love yourself, just as you are, without rescuing or helping Shirley or anyone else?

IC: I am not sure. How would I do that?

IS: Could you relax some of your rules and expectations about what loving people can and cannot do?

IC: Yes, I can do that.

IS: Great. Can you also forgive yourself for having judged yourself as being a bad person for not living up to unreasonable expectations of yourself?

IC: I think I can, yes. That feels much better now. Thank you.

IS: Great pleasure. Any time. Remember I am always here for you.

What you are aiming for with this dialogue is to bring healing into the areas that hurt through receiving forgiveness. It is an action of both giving and receiving, essentially within yourself, and is best completed with as light a touch as possible so that you give the wounds the maximum opportunity for healing. Experiment for yourself and discover the benefits of doing this exercise.

Rewriting the Intention in your Heart

Essentially, when we forgive we are forgiving ourselves for our misinterpretation of events. There is a saying which goes:

If we knew the secret hurts of our worst enemies, we would do nothing further to harm them, in thought, word or action.

Have you ever found yourself mentally turning your negative thoughts about yourself **(I)** or others **(O)** around in your head, almost as a means of justifying yourself or your point of view? This kind of anxiety can keep us awake at night, when it becomes even more distorted. The spiralling-down effect takes place as negative thoughts chase negative emotions. As already mentioned, if not arrested and resolved, these hurts can become buried in the depths of memory, from where they may subsequently surface to obscure the accurate perception of ourselves (**I**), others (**O**) or the events we encounter.

There is a positive alternative to burying and hiding your hurts. First of all, you need to be *aware* of your negative thinking. Your body will issue an early warning system, because negative thoughts producing negative emotion will cause some form of stress. It may seem simplistic, but the act of changing your thoughts will produce a change of experience.

The 'catch' here perhaps is that a habit of negative thinking does not get changed overnight. Like conquering any other addiction, effecting a positive change is a matter of taking one step at a time and gradually laying down a new track of positivity. It also means letting go of the assumption that we can foretell the future based upon our experience of the past. This takes a courageous heart, willing to sacrifice a false sense of security and control to embrace the possibilities, right now, of creating a better future experience.

You may be familiar with the idea of 'self-fulfilling prophecy' and the biblical:

> As a man thinketh, in his heart so he becomes.

A forgiving heart is one that is free from the burden of assuming control over circumstances which are fundamentally 'out of control'.

Our minds and emotions are like a running motor which often cannot be switched off at will. Running negatively is like having a gear in reverse, taking you over old ground. With, as it were, the clutch of awareness, you can shift into positive gear, and drive in the new direction you would prefer. The gear, your choice of direction, is in your hands and heart.

A forgiving attitude facilitates the gear shift from reverse into advance. This attitude can be created by statements of forgiveness. They are something you can do, almost mechanically, until the meaning they have can drop into place for you. The word 'judging' used in the following exercise is not the neutral sense of discernment but the restrictive energy of one of those subjective negative emotions such as fear, anger, doubt, confusion, criticism and self-righteousness.

Statements of Forgiveness

You might like to experiment with forming your own statements of forgiveness until you arrive at whatever falls into place for you. You can repeat them inwardly if you like. After each statement, you might like to take in a deep breath, relax and let the breath out, allowing yourself to feel more peaceful as you do so.

This exercise may be best done to begin with by writing the statements down and allowing a spontaneous flow to happen, allowing your thoughts to come forward freely. Our judgements are often locked into our unconscious makeup and form our defences against the world.

Start with the statement:

I forgive myself for judging myself or any other being or situation, consciously or unconsciously.

Then continue with whatever personal transgressions or judgements come to mind, for example:

♥ I forgive myself for judging myself for feeling resentful towards Mary.

♥ I forgive myself for judging Harry as being very stupid.

♥ I forgive myself for judging Susan for losing her temper.

♥ I forgive myself for judging the action of the teachers union in schools.

♥ I forgive myself for judging politicians as being dishonest.

♥ I forgive myself for shouting at Chris.

♥ I forgive myself for hating my step-father.

♥ I forgive myself for judging myself for hating my step-father. Etc.

Ideally, we might approach life totally accepting and uncritical of any aspect of it – in which case, we would have no need to forgive ourselves. We can by all means learn to be more selective in choosing the people and situations that we entertain. It is by projecting **(I)** or **(O)** the negative emotions of our *critical attitudes*, however subtle, that we wound ourselves. Therefore, the more we can promote a forgiving attitude towards ourselves and the whole of the process of life around us, the more peaceful we will be.

Any time in the future when you catch yourself in a judgemental frame of mind, experiment with a variety of forgiveness statements and observe how you can miraculously change your frame of mind and feel freer. Repeating those statements of forgiveness is a way of promoting within yourself a forgiving attitude.

From Distance to Intimacy (I)

Peace is primarily an inner, or intimate, experience hard to describe verbally to anyone else. However, we can organize the immediate world around us to enhance that inner experience. We cannot change other people or events, but we can stay in charge of, or be accountable for, those areas of our lives with which we have a direct relationship. This boils down to completing what we have undertaken to do.

While this looks very simple – and it is – the process of

following through on what we have agreed can be subject to abuse in many, often unconscious ways. Inwardly, it is due to the non-cooperation of the Inner Child, possibly because we have taken too great a burden upon ourselves. So lack of ease or peace in your life could be a result of undertaking more than you can reasonably manage, perhaps even attempting to lead other people's lives for them. In this case, in order to gain approval or acceptance from others whom you care about, you may take on commitments for them that you are not able to fulfil clearly. This could result in your feeling guilty for not successfully meeting the commitments, and resentful towards the other person, or people, for having 'forced' you into the agreement in the first place. In expressing our love and caring for others, we need to find the balance between active involvement and allowing them freedom to live, learn and grow from their own experiences.

The balancing point, your intuitive sense of knowing, can be found within your intimate centre of peace, to which only you have access. The following guided visualization will assist you to reach your inner peace.

Receiving your Peace

This is a guided visualization, so, again, you might like to record it so that you can listen to it entirely with your eyes closed or read one section, then close your eyes to reflect inwardly on the images that come forward. Either way, make sure that you are in as quiet and undisturbed a place as you can be.

Take in a deep breath . . . Let it out very gently and gradually . . . Take in another deep breath . . . and as you let this out envisage yourself being surrounded by the most beautiful colours . . . purest sounds . . . softest winds that caress your skin . . .

Feel yourself being lifted high above the world you normally inhabit . . . You might envisage an aircraft or a spaceship of some kind . . . horses pulling a regal carriage . . . or growing wings of magic . . .

Allow yourself to be transported to an extraordinary world of peace and plenty . . . All the dreams you have ever dreamed are here for you . . . And there are others here . . . simply having fun . . . You notice the kindness and freedom with which they interact . . . There is an absence of pressure . . . and an abundance of respect . . . You are also aware of the agelessness of each being . . . such is the freshness . . . the freedom . . . the vitality being expressed . . .

One person comes towards you now . . . with such bright and clear eyes that you feel drawn in that direction . . . Of all the images . . . dreams . . . scenarios you have seen in this world, the person asks you which you would like to take back with you to the world you currently inhabit . . .

And there is one vision . . . of exquisite harmony, balance and beauty that makes its presence known to you now . . . It is this vision that you would like to experience more fully in your everyday life . . .

The person invites you to enter into the vision . . . to make it your own . . . to live it . . . to enjoy it . . . to know it in every cell of your being . . . to feel the nurturing impact that it has for your growth and evolvement right now . . . Receive this fullness of who you are . . . Know the radiant quality of your peace . . .

Express your gratitude in any way that you wish . . . envisage the words . . . hear the feeling communicate itself into this world . . .

With this radiant quality still vibrant . . . gently return yourself to your immediate world . . . open your eyes when you are ready . . . become aware of your hands and feet . . . your hands through which you give . . . and receive . . . your feet that carry you forward in your life's progression . . .

Look with the eyes of gratitude as you become more fully aware of the world in which you live . . . You do not have to do anything . . . Each breath you take is a breath of grace . . . the grace that is enabling you to receive . . . to return to a happy state beyond your wildest imaginings . . .

You might like to take a pen and notebook and record any impressions you experienced during the visualization. What were the insights you might be able to incorporate into your relationships now? What are the keys to your peace?

Growing from Grief to Gratitude

Whenever we encounter any emotional challenge within a relationship, **(I)** or **(O)**, we might view it as a door leading towards a deeper appreciation of the strengths and qualities with which we were born. Passing through the doorway may involve us in an experience of loss before we awaken, with gratitude, to the gain on the other side. As we pass through, as we detach ourselves from familiar habits and patterns of thought or behaviour, we may experience the stress and pain associated with grief.

The most painful grief to bear may come with the death of a parent, spouse or other close loved one. This may be the greatest emotional crisis we ever encounter. The Chinese cryptograph for crisis holds the meaning of both 'danger' and 'opportunity'. The danger might be that we remain attached to our feelings of loss and grief; the opportunity might be that we can further awaken to the loving within ourselves **(I)** that was reflected in the lost relationship **(O)**. Our loving is the foundation for the sadness experienced and the tears expressed through grief.

It is held in some schools of thought that our attachments are the cause of our suffering. Yet it is a natural part of our human lot to experience attachment to those we love. The emptiness experienced in loss can only be refilled inwardly **(I)**, never by replacing the outer object of our affections.

Our reluctance **(I)** to confront the grief associated with loss and letting go of attachments, however, may inhibit us from stepping free from the limiting patterns and habits in our relationships **(O)**, from walking through the doorway into a greater experience of happiness and fulfilment. But one of the keys that can open the door to your increased happiness is your own self-esteem – which it is in your power (I) to enhance.

One method of building your self-esteem is to do whatever 'work' (in the broadest meaning of the word) honours your sense of values – and then remember it. You may just make a mental note of what you have achieved or, if you have a tendency to doubt yourself, it might be better to write down in a place where you will see it from time to time, a list of your accomplishments.

This kind of acknowledgment to and appreciation of yourself fills your personal well of self-esteem and opens you to receive more (I) and (O). As you receive more, so you can, if you choose, give back (O) in greater ways than before. You may find that you do not need to rush out in pursuit of new avenues of giving. The opportunities may simply present themselves in ways that are easy and simple for you to fulfil.

Your may find then that your inner peace begins to come, hand in hand with the recognition of your inherent goodness (I). Our experience of peace nestles within that innate goodness.

Listening – A Key to the Door of your Peace

The greatest wealth you can ever enjoy is that with which you were born. It is there patiently waiting for you to reveal it to yourself. Rather like a door that opens out towards you, pressure and force against it will not enable it to move so that you can walk in to the treasures behind it.

So if we cannot open the door to our peace through our will-power, charisma and personal force, what is left to us? While we patiently wait outside that door and meanwhile go about our daily activities, we can nurture our capacity for fun and enjoyment, laughter and loving **(I)** and **(O)**. With a light frame of mind, we can more easily hear, as we listen for it, the still small voice of our peace **(I)** when it beckons us.

Chapter 4

Expansion

. . . Winning in All Ways

In order to experience **(I)** greater happiness and fulfilment in your relationships with others **(O)**, you will need to grow through some of the boundaries and limitations that have formerly held you in restraint, and make some positive moves to go beyond them. This is easier said than done, or you would have already taken the necessary action. In the last chapter we started breaking down barriers **(I)**, gaining access to your creative potential for increased happiness. This chapter will suggest many ways of taking simple steps **(I) > (O)** in whatever may be your most challenging relationships with others **(O)**.

Your Journey Outwards

Before you embark upon a journey, you need to have a good idea of your destination so that you can set a direction. You may never have visited Bombay before, for example, but you can know where it is on the map and select suitable transport to get you there.

The fuel for your journey outwards **(O)** will be the loving energy in your 'heart' **(I)**, perhaps most easily recognized in qualities such as courage, integrity, clarity and strength of purpose. It is qualities such as these that will enable you to confront the limitations within you **(I)**, expand your loving expression towards others **(O)** and then experience the expansion within you **(I)**.

The final destination that you are choosing, the experience **(I)** and expression **(O)** of greater loving, is likely to be very similar to that of both your friends and adversaries. Your starting-point, methods of transportation and stops along the way may well differ. No matter what differences you experience in your relationships **(O)**, your travelling companions are ultimately heading for the same location.

This is important to bear in mind when determining an objective within a relationship which is important to you. In confronting and surrendering your own limitations, you need to allow for an outcome in which others also experience a benefit. There is no room for revenge. If you seek to gain or take something out of a relationship in such a way that the other person suffers, the loser is the relationship. The way to 'win' **(I)** is that which serves the greatest good of all **(O)**.

Abandon your 'Rights' (O) and Go for the Value (I)

One of the greatest, often unseen, barriers that we erect to limit our capacity for happiness is a self-righteous attitude. The 'I am right, you are wrong' stand, about even small household matters, creates distance and separation **(I)**. Where two or more could come together to resolve an issue, a single one clinging to an opinion freezes the possibility for any creative solution. The self-righteous attitude **(I)** becomes a prison of defences within which you, essentially, become the greatest loser.

Would you rather be 'right' or happy? As you are able to let go of the need to be 'right' in your opinions and drop the barricades to your loving, you can more fully receive the extraordinary, fundamental value in your own life, and in the lives of others. Surrendering your weapons, or leaving the battlefield, are just two choices you have in order to achieve greater happiness.

Perceiving **(I)** the value in ourselves and others takes place inwardly with an open and receptive frame of mind. Whether you or anyone else *behaves* less than well, the intrinsic value **(I)** remains. Within you, it is dormant until you choose to act **(O)** and awaken it more fully in your awareness **(I)**. Your greatest value is in the awareness of your loving, but you will not find it through fighting, **(I)** or **(O)**. When you can seize those opportunities to know yourself more fully as a loving person, you will find it more worthwhile than words can describe.

The First Steps

What if your ultimate aim, the final destination, were that of perpetual, unconditional loving? You could probably identify a relationship **(O)** not too far away from you in which to initiate the process of loving expansion. In fact, the closer that relationship is to you, i.e. the greater the emotional content, the greater the challenge and opportunity of experiencing an increase in the quality of your loving. The greater the barrier, the greater the breakthrough.

The first step to work with is that of the perception of yourself **(I)** within that relationship **(O)**. Perception is really no more than a point of view. So fresh information can dramatically change it – and remove limitations. You can be so close to a situation that you 'cannot see the wood for the trees'. As tree huggers, we lose sight of the forest and the oceans of opportunity beyond. Likewise, when we cling to our judgements of ourselves **(I)** or others **(O)**, we may fail to recognize the creative moves available to us. It might be helpful to take a step back and look at things from a new viewpoint.

As a starting-point, it is worth working out specifically what it is you most want within a relationship. This can often then raise all kinds of doubts and fears about whether you can really have it. Often, it feels safer and more secure to stick with what you have got because you fear it may be the best that you can hope to expect. We tend to resist change **(I) + (O)** and are reluctant to rock the boat, even if there are holes in the hull and we are constantly baling out.

Baling ourselves out of the relationship is of course an option in some circumstances if we cannot, for any reason, apply our loving resources to maintain ourselves within it. We may choose to cease communication with a parent or child, or to divorce a spouse. This is always an option, but it may be more beneficial to take steps to improve the relationship first.

If you were to identify an improvement within a relationship, you might well expect the other person to be responsible for it. But we only meet with disappointment when we indulge in wishful thinking about how things might be different – 'if only they . . .' – then do nothing ourselves and expect the other person not only to read our minds, but also take the action we want **(I)** without our having communicated it **(O)**. If we give up responsibility for ourselves like this, we can only expect frustration. Even if the other person is doing their utmost for us, they can never completely fill in the gaps **(O)** that only we **(I)** can know about.

Knowing what you want within a relationship comes down to how you view yourself experiencing that relationship **(I)**, *contributing* **(O)** to it in ways that work for you. You may first of all know what you do *not* want and can eliminate that, before discovering what you *do* want.

(As mentioned earlier, you may not want the entire relationship.) As you clarify a positive focus or direction for yourself **(I)**, you can begin to align your attitudes, action and behaviour **(O)** to produce the experiences **(I)** you want.

Consider your Options

To look at the available options for your expansion, consider the following:

1. Your first option is whether to participate in a relationship or not. There may be any number of obligatory factors that enter here, such as those of caring for a dependent, elderly relative. In other words, it may seem as though the choice is being made for you. It may be a sense of guilt, imposed by yourself or others, that would prevent you from choosing not to participate in such a relationship.

2. Once you choose to participate in a relationship, your best option is that of nurturing the most positive attitudes towards yourself and the other person at a level that comes as close to 100 per cent commitment as you can achieve. The 100 per cent does not refer to your level of performance in terms of being the most loving person around in difficult situations. It refers to your willingness to participate and learn how to love, **(I) + (O)**, when the choices are not obvious. There may be occasions when you do less than your best and recognize it as such. Rather than castigate yourself for your errors, look at them with loving and learn from them until you find how to stay on your positive track.

3. For whatever reason, you may choose not to participate in a relationship. The discomfort you experience with a certain person may be greater than you wish to endure. Yet the prospect of leaving a relationship that no longer

supports you may throw up a spectre of even greater discomfort. The best relationship begins with yourself and only you can know the course you need to take.

4. If you are choosing to let go of a relationship, then you need to find a way of terminating it that is most honourable, in the sense of the loving consideration you extend towards yourself and the other person. Alternatively, you may wish to change some aspect of the form of the relationship, letting go of certain habitual patterns within it **(I)** that are destructive for you.

Knowing What You Want (I)

For this exercise, choose a relationship **(O)** that is important for you. It could be with a parent, child, step-parent/child, in-law, spouse, employer or any close partnership.

With this relationship in mind, you can start to draw a 'mind map', allowing questions to surface in your mind and writing them down as they occur. As the creative mind thinks by association, not by linear logical progression, mind mapping is a good method for releasing doubts and concerns. If not aired, these will limit the awareness of your loving. When known, they can be used to enhance your expansion.

A mind map will enable you to become clear about what you already know about a subject and where there are gaps in your knowledge. In the centre of the mind map, write your objective for the exercise and surround it with a border. Extending out from the border, written on lines of free association, your mind can then deliver all the thoughts you currently hold about the objective. Be spontaneous and do not censor any thought as being inappropriate. You can be as daring and outrageous as you like.

For example, write in the centre,

 'Knowing what I want with . . . .'

and put the name of the person. Figure 8 illustrates how your mind map could look.

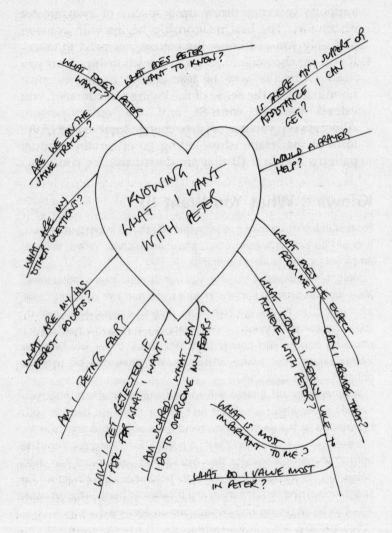

Figure 8: Knowing what you want – mind map.

When you have completed the mind map you will notice that one or more of the questions will offer you some direction, even if it is a clear decision not to do anything for the moment. Just having brought the questions to mind, you will begin unconsciously to resolve them and get in touch with what you want.

Learning, Healing and Integration

The Peace Cycle from the last chapter has another dimension, which is that of a spiral upwards into a level of greater well-being, of increasing confidence. Greater confidence is the reward that comes from embracing difficulties, expanding your awareness **(I)** within a relationship and taking positive action **(O)**.

A *Spiral of Increasing Confidence* might also be seen as a *Spiral of Learning, Healing and Integration*. When we encounter difficulties, rather than berate ourselves and others, we might stand back to look towards the source of our upset **(I)**. We may then discover the opportunity of learning and healing **(I)** being offered to us through the relationship **(O)**. An attitude of gratitude towards our loved ones for the challenges they present to us will assist us in achieving what we most want. In the heat of the moment, this may not be as easy as it sounds. But, over time, it is well worth nurturing a greater sense of gratitude.

Your reluctance, or enthusiasm, for expansion will be largely affected by the degree of co-operation you attain with your Inner Child. It is here, in the relationship with your Child **(I)**, that you can begin to develop the strength and trust that will make the difference to your interactions with others. If in any way you lack clarity or confidence in your relationships **(O)**, the source of your difficulty is likely to be found in your Inner Child.

Communication is important here, as 'mixed messages', either **(I)** or **(O)**, will result in 'mixed' results, or results that you would rather not have. When you know clearly what you want, what you value and is most important to you, you can negotiate from the heart in a direct way that will touch the heart of the other person (I) > (O). He/she is then free make the choice whether to participate with you or not. Either way, you are both clear and avoid unnecessary confusion.

Beyond the Shadow of a Doubt

While many of us would like to derive greater pleasure in our relationships and enjoy the benefits of increased confidence and communication, we are often held in check. Concealed from our conscious awareness are those doubts which cast a shadow across the picture of what we really want.

Uncertainty or doubt (I) in our capacity for loving or being lovable is at the root of our difficulties in relationships (O). But, as mentioned earlier, with awareness, doubts can lead to expansion.

Our sense of doubt may have been created by our experiences of the past, particularly the painful and difficult ones. We may lack confidence that we are lovable and worthwhile. At its deepest point, self-doubt is a final rejection of the loving within ourselves and is distressing. When we deny that loving within us, we often seek outside sources to fill in the gaps or emptiness. This can lead to the formation of many kinds of dependency and to the attempt to exert control over others. We depend on these outside sources either for what we think they can give *to* us, or for what we feel they need *from* us. A possessive mother is an example of such a relationship. But if you reject the loving within you (I), it is likely that you will also experience rejection in your outer relationships (O).

With expansion, however, this downward spiral of

suffering associated with attachment, control and dependency could be surrendered and replaced with a free and happy acceptance of the variety of human expressions, especially of those closest to us. The expanded vision might be one in which we are able to give of ourselves freely, simply for the joy of giving, without the dependency of needing or expecting any return whatsoever.

The movement from doubt to expansion is one that we can develop over time. The *Triangle of Trust* (see Chapter 2, page 68) can be employed for this. For the purposes of expansion, we shall be making doubt, self-denial and rejection a thing of the *past*. The direction we are moving towards is that of an expansion of the quality of loving **(I)** + **(O)** and the freedom associated with it in the *future*. We can do nothing to change the past. Right now, we can establish fresh choices, plan and prepare for the future we would like to enjoy. Past events may be part of our unchangeable history, but they do not have to be a burden to us right now if we can break out of the pattern of *attitude, belief, action or behaviour* that led us to negative experiences. *Right now* we have the possibility of making a *fresh choice* and one that will lead to an improved experience. This may be a matter of 'trial and error' but it can be treated as an adventure or experiment. Nothing ventured, as the saying goes, nothing gained.

Working the three sides of the *Triangle of Trust* with your Inner Child, you can *expand* the experience **(I)** and expression of loving through your relationships **(O)**. Remember that your Child needs to feel safe from criticism, unthreatened, if an experimental new behaviour or action does not produce the best result. Importantly, he or she needs to be acknowledged for being willing to co-operate and take the risk in the first place. But he or she will receive encouragement when, having undertaken the experiment, you promise *and then deliver* a treat or reward.

You may be in a challenging relationship with a person

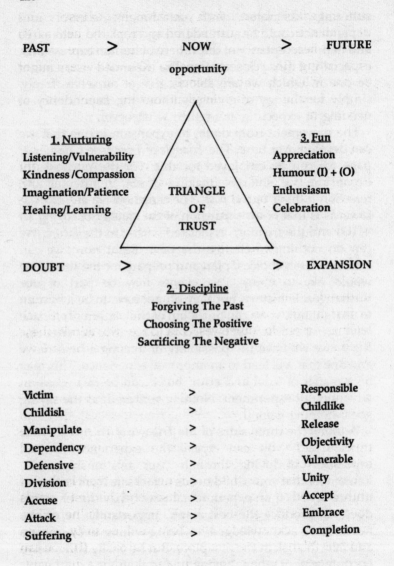

PAST > NOW > FUTURE

opportunity

1. Nurturing
Listening/Vulnerability
Kindness /Compassion
Imagination/Patience
Healing/Learning

TRIANGLE
OF
TRUST

3. Fun
Appreciation
Humour (I) + (O)
Enthusiasm
Celebration

DOUBT > > EXPANSION

2. Discipline
Forgiving The Past
Choosing The Positive
Sacrificing The Negative

Victim	>	Responsible
Childish	>	Childlike
Manipulate	>	Release
Dependency	>	Objectivity
Defensive	>	Vulnerable
Division	>	Unity
Accuse	>	Accept
Attack	>	Embrace
Suffering	>	Completion

Figure 9: Doubt – the way out to expansion.

able and willing to work with you through your insecurities or doubts. If not, you can still bring about the healing **(I)** and **(O)** because as you learn to awaken to more of your own loving **(I)**, your relationship **(O)** with every other person will automatically benefit.

Let's look in greater detail at moving from doubt to expansion.

1. Nurturing

Perhaps the greatest gift we can give ourselves and our loved ones is that of our time. That time can potentially be mutually nurturing. The aim of expansion in this area is that of emotional maturity. Emotional maturity takes place as we integrate those aspects of ourselves which were blocked, or denied, in the course of our growing up.

In order to receive **(I)** the nurturing we need, we must first admit our feelings of vulnerability. We may 'protect' underlying self-doubt by expressing anger and aggression, or fear and defensiveness, rather than dare to admit such feelings, even to ourselves. But once we admit these uncomfortable truths, we can begin to receive the care we deserve.

Similarly, in order to nurture our loved ones **(O)**, we need to communicate to them that it is safe for them to be vulnerable with us. If you are bullying or critical, they will feel threatened and so will shut down and not be in a position to receive what you have to give, however well intentioned that may be.

The underlying expression of nurturing then is that of kindness and compassion. You can extend this first towards yourself **(I)** as you get in touch with your own vulnerability, creating an experience of safety and security within yourself. With a greater sense of personal safety **(I)**, you can then extend your compassion and kindness into your relationships by being open and receptive to the needs **(O)** of others. *Listen* for your opportunities of expansion.

Expansion can come at those times when we are brought into conflict with those we love and care for the most **(O)**. These are likely to be opportunities to examine deeply hidden self-doubts **(I)**. We generally bury such doubts beneath the surface, hoping they will not be discovered, rather than confront them, but they can eat away at the fibre of our being. In a conflict, it is typically much 'easier' to project blame for the upset on the one who apparently 'caused' it, rather than examine the inner cause of the hurt. But ideally, the best way of releasing the doubt is to reveal it to the other person as an honest statement about how you are feeling, in such a way that they are not made to be at fault.

It is, however, possible that over a period of years, your doubts may have stockpiled on each other, compounding layers of confusion, so that it is not possible to communicate clearly the issue involved. In this case, the charity, or caring, begins at home, within you **(I)**. You can release negative energy of the doubt through free-form writing. Whether you are experiencing the emotions of anger or depression or both, sitting down with a pen and pad of paper and writing out whatever comes to mind, without censoring any of it, is a good start in getting at the truth behind the upset. Do not reread anything that you have written out. Releasing means letting go of it, so do that completely. Destroy the written pages however you wish.

This is a way in which you can listen to yourself and initiate the process of self-healing **(I)**, which in turn will ultimately bring balance into those outer relationships **(O)**.

Negative emotions are sticky, heavy and glutinous. As long as your energies are negatively oriented, your 'issues' will stick to you, layer upon layer if you let them, until you en*light*en yourself. Positive emotions will free you. So, treat yourself as you mean to go on, with as *light* a touch as you can manage.

Vulnerability – Your Key to Creativity

When you are most in touch with your vulnerability, you are at a turning point when you can choose either to sink into misery or to swim to the shore. The way you can begin to nurture yourself **(I)** through your relationships with others **(O)** is by envisaging the quality of experience and expression you would most like. The gift of your imagination is the starting point.

In this exercise you will be using a specific close relationship in which you experience a certain lack of ease to assist you in defining a more positive result. You will be creating an ideal scene and, for the purpose of this exercise, do not dwell in a doubt. Although the difficulty may appear great, it may only take a relatively small initial adjustment to effect the first improvement. A journey of 1,000 miles begins with the first step.

It is important to remember that your main fields of growth and expansion will be *within yourself*. Others will ultimately benefit from the nurturing you extend towards yourself. As your own capacity for fulfilment increases, you may well find yourself letting go of less than satisfactory relationships and welcoming others that more closely match your own growth.

If a negative expectation surfaces in your mind, turn it into a positive statement. Give yourself permission to fling open the doors of possibility.

As you create your ideal scene, allow your imagination to stimulate your feelings of enthusiasm. Have fun breaking through your rules of limitation and lack. Imagine you live in a world in which anything is possible, miracles are the order of the day and magical solutions are available to your greatest difficulties. Paint the picture of your dreams.

Bear in mind the statements concerning happiness you made earlier (see page 42). You can also refer to the *Guidelines for Making Affirmations* (page 30). Remember that you are in charge of how you experience your relationships. Your attitudes, actions and behaviour will influence your experience.

The first part of this exercise will be a walk with your Inner Child in which you have the opportunity to listen to his/her heartfelt wishes for your relationships. This is a visualization which you may wish to record to listen to entirely with your eyes closed. You will need a pen and paper at the end of the visualization.

Take in a deep breath, place your hand over your abdomen and, as you breathe out, envisage loving being radiated to your Child. Let the Child know he/she is safe and secure, free to express whatever he/she wants. Take some more deep breaths until you feel warm, relaxed and receptive.

Imagine yourself on a perfect day in which the air is clear . . . You can feel the sun's gentle warmth on your skin and hear the sparkling sounds of birds and insects . . . Find yourself in nature with your Inner Child by your side, holding your hand . . . Ask if there is anywhere he/she would particularly like to go . . . to a stream perhaps . . . into a forest . . . onto a beach . . . to the top of a tree . . . to the centre of a tropical island . . . See yourself there . . . now . . .

Take a few moments to ask your Child about any relationship that has been challenging for you . . . Above all, listen to what your Child would ideally like to have happen . . . Ask about the experience you would most like to be having . . . if anything were possible . . . Take some time to simply listen . . . and hear the voice of your Child . . .

Wherever you are now . . . imagine a huge screen . . . Envisage yourself up on that screen interacting with the person with whom you have a challenging relationship . . . in a way that works for both of you . . . Notice how you feel inside as you observe the ease of the interaction in front of you . . .

What are those qualities that you are now experiencing . . .? Breathe into them . . . and observe how they expand and fill every cell in your body . . .

With those qualities of fullness vibrantly within you . . . turn to your Inner Child and embrace him/her with gratitude for working so well with you . . . let your Child know of your loving and appreciation . . .

Keep those positive qualities radiantly within you as you pick up the pen and paper and make any notes that you would like to recall details of the visualization.

Referring to those notes if you wish, draw up an ideal scene in statement form of the relationship that has been challenging for you. Each statement is framed positively as if it is happening right now for you. The following questions may assist you in clarifying points of expansion.

♥ Do you feel safe to express yourself with this person?
♥ Are you happy to be open and listen to this person effectively?
♥ Is the quality of intimacy as you would wish it?
♥ Is the time you spend with this person productive for you?
♥ Do you have as much fun together as you would like?
♥ How can you renegotiate your limiting expectations and expand your beliefs and attitudes in the relationship?
♥ What is the most loving communication you have yet to make?
♥ If the relationship is romantic, do you enjoy the quality of sexual expression and experience that you would like?
♥ If there were an absence of fear or anger in the relationship, how would you behave more lovingly?
♥ What personal assets, strengths and qualities do you have that you can express more fully in your relationship?
♥ How will you acknowledge yourself for risking new positive behaviour?
♥ What other components do you need to complete this ideal scene in the relationship you would now like to be enjoying more fully?

The following example illustrates an ideal scene:

The relationship is with a close friend I grew up with, who is like a sister to me.

♥ I remain relaxed and confident in her presence.
♥ I feel safe expressing my concerns with her.
♥ I am happy to be quiet in her company.
♥ All my actions support my positive vision.
♥ I find many interesting ways of showing how much I care for her.

♥ My attitudes are opening me to new possibilities in sharing the love we have for each other.

♥ I am happy asking for what I want and being open to receive.

♥ I feel loved, cared for and supported.

♥ It is easy for me to accept her differing points of view on Christianity.

♥ I discover greater qualities of trust opening up for me.

♥ It is fun for me to replace limiting behaviour with loving actions.

♥ My new levels of loving expression and experience build my sense of self-esteem in extraordinary ways.

♥ As I expand in this relationship, my confidence increases in leaps and bounds.

Nurturing yourself with a positive vision is the first step to expanding within a challenging relationship. You could also set an ideal scene when you embark on a new significant relationship, or are simply at a turning point of an existing one. Remember your ideal scene, write it down, keep it in a private place and refer to it often.

Each time you read through the ideal scene, you might choose one specific action **(I)** or **(O)** to take to reinforce or enhance one aspect of it. It could be an act of kindness, a statement of forgiveness, a loving word, a letter of appreciation. Any positive step you take will be nurturing and rewarding for you. Be creative and take as many as you need until you arrive at your ideal scene, or one that is even better than you had imagined.

You can do this with more than one relationship if you wish. Also, the ideal scene that you envisage today could be modified over time. Once a year, you may wish to review and revise your ideal scenes, acknowledging your accomplishments and growth, setting new visions for improvement and expansion.

Avoid, however, setting dates for achieving your visions. Some aspects of your vision may fall into place tomorrow. Others may take time and practice before you learn how to replace self-sabotage with self-support and fulfil your aims.

2. Discipline

The choices we exercise over our thoughts and actions will influence, positively or negatively, how we feel and the level of energy or vitality we have available to us. Our capacity for making wise choices **(I)** forms the foundation for our fulfilment in relationships **(O)**. Indecision, or lack of commitment, makes for a shaky inner foundation on which to create the conditions of greater happiness.

The discipline that leads to expansion is about making the *loving choices* that honour both yourself and others close to you. Developing daily clarity of thought, word and action in your relationships is as demanding as the physical training and preparation for a marathon or similar sporting event.

Having a detailed, expanded vision in mind, and on paper, sets a focus towards which you can direct yourself. This is more than simply a matter of positive or negative *thinking*. Thoughts by themselves come and go and we never have any control over them moment by moment. Having a well-defined *aim* gives you a focal point towards which to direct yourself. Before you arrive, you may well take some wrong turnings, make some mistakes, which seem counter-productive, and think or feel discouraged. The value of having an aim is that even when you are *feeling* doubtful, or *thinking* negatively, you can still refocus on your chosen target and consider now what you need to do differently to achieve what you want.

Once you are aware of an error in your approach, you can correct your course with a minimum of fuss by refreshing yourself with the vision, and taking the next step. The only mistake perhaps would be to give up in discouragement before you arrive. If *en route* you fall short of your vision, this is not the end of the world. As the song goes, pick yourself up, dust yourself down and start all over again.

When you are pulling together in your relationships **(O)**, the inner wealth you can experience **(I)** will astound you.

Loving discipline **(I)** leads to self-healing. This healing will then communicate itself to your loved ones and **(O)** contribute to their lives.

Do not be put off by the word 'discipline'. In the past you may have experienced discipline as being harsh or punishment-oriented, as something imposed from without **(O)** and linked to personal deprivation, withdrawal of love, approval or privilege. But *self-determined discipline* **(I)** is more a matter of choosing a clear way of positive self-support, being happy and willing to sacrifice the habits that led to your hurting. It is a reward-oriented approach. Treating yourself with firmness, kindness and compassion is naturally rewarding. Exercise discipline in this way and you will automatically feel better within yourself **(I)** and enjoy greater freedom in your relationships with others **(O)**.

Forgive – And Be Blessed

You may well find that as you become clearer about what you really want **(O)**, you become more aware of the emotional debris and clutter **(I)** in the way of your achieving it. Incidents that you thought were long since dead and buried may surface. Achieving what you want is simply a matter of clearing up old issues from the past **(I)**, and taking action **(O)** in the direction of your vision. Simple, not necessarily easy.

You may find that it is not until you have chosen to break free from your limitations that you recognize those conditions **(I)** which may be the most entrenched, and those issues, **(I)** and **(O)**, that you most need to forgive. Look back over the last chapter to remind yourself of the benefits of learning to forgive (pages 104–7).

Forgiving yourself is important, as effecting positive changes within relationships is challenging both inwardly to yourself and outwardly to those others with whom you have fallen into certain familiar patterns of behaviour. Also, instead of warmly welcoming improvement and change, many of us emotionally resist and fight it, even when rationally we know that what is happening is 'for the best'. The process of change can make us feel upset and then on top of that we can feel bad about feeling upset. Rationally and emotionally, we seem to be at odds with ourselves. We may also (irrationally) extend that inner conflict out towards others, usually whoever happens to be closest to us.

Exercising forgiveness, as mentioned in the last chapter, brings the mind and emotions into greater alignment and harmony. As you forgive yourself, or anyone else, for the perceived transgressions, and receive the loving of that forgiveness, you bring about tremendous growth and healing in your capacity for perception **(I)**.

From our limited human perspective, we may criticize. From our loving human perspective, we also have the capacity to forgive. When we choose the loving option, we become open to receive many blessings.

Clearing the Way with Forgiving

This exercise is one in which you can pinpoint any negative experience you have had and release it through forgiving. You may be forgiving someone else, although finally you are always forgiving yourself. The negativity you *hold against* anyone else **(O)**, forms part of the debris within you **(I)** that will limit you from the quality of life you would most like.

This is not to say you can never have a negative feeling or thought towards yourself or others in order to experience fulfilment in your relationships. The choice you have is either to let it churn around inside of you, breeding discontent, or to let it go, forgive and forget it.

You will need a pen and paper to write out statements of forgiveness (see *Statements of Forgiveness* exercise, page 109), this time concerning those against whom you have held prolonged negativity, resentment or bitterness.

First of all, bring to mind again what it is you would like to be enjoying more in a close relationship that has been challenging to you. As you review your positive aims, you may recall incidents from the past, still painful for you now, in which you felt hurt, let down, disappointed, betrayed or misunderstood. Unresolved hurts from the past will lessen your capacity for loving in present and future relationships.

The following are examples of the kinds of relationship experiences which you may have yet to forgive:

♥ Your father falling in love with a younger, prettier woman and leaving your mother to live with her.
♥ Your mother giving more love and attention to a favourite brother/sister.
♥ Resentment towards a step-mother or step-father.
♥ Your uncle sexually molesting you when you were three.
♥ Hatred towards an interfering mother-in-law.
♥ A parent's drunken and abusive behaviour.
♥ Your father making his work more important than his family.
♥ Your lover abandoning you for your best friend.

If none of these fits your particular picture, consider anything that someone has done to you that is 'unforgivable'. That is what you must now forgive.

The unforgivable I now willingly forgive.

Put aside any doubts, lingering reluctance and write out that first statement of forgiveness, *as if* you were emotionally ready to forgive that which you considered unforgivable. Writing out forgiveness statements ten times is a first step to laying in a new positive track for your present and future happiness.

For example:

♥ I forgive Dad for beating up Mum when he used to get back from the bar.

♥ I forgive Mum for withholding the loving I wanted from her.

Even if, emotionally, your statement does not fall into place for you immediately, it is worth taking the time to work with it until it does. With persistence and an open mind, you can alleviate many inbuilt pressures with forgiveness.

You may have more than one upsetting incident that you are still holding, especially from when you were young and most impressionable. There may be some that you chose to hide from your consciousness. As you begin to heal, balance and clear those old wounds, expanding more fully into your loving resources, layers of injury will surface gradually so that, one by one, you can turn former limitations to new strengths. Be patient and gentle with yourself.

Do this exercise now as an important step towards healing yourself **(I)**, and any future relationships **(O)** in which former hurts limit your present capacity for loving.

The Path of Perfect Parenthood

One area in which we may have to forgive ourselves and others is our childhood and parenting experiences. Perfect parenthood does not exist, not as we normally conceive of it. The notion that perfection does exist is the basis for continuing confusion in the relationships with ourselves **(I)** and others **(O)**.

All parents embark upon an impossible venture if they even aim to be 'perfect'. On the one hand, they take on the responsibility, one way or another, for offering discipline, guidance and direction for life, and on the other hand, they gave birth to a 'teacher' who is likely to test them to the limits of their endurance. There may be no such thing as the perfect parent, but then, is there ever a 'perfect child'?

While we may have inherited our patterns of negativity, or limitation, from our parents, it is detrimental to our health to 'point the finger of blame' at them for how we currently experience our relationships. When we blame *anyone else* for how we feel now, we discharge responsibility and personal power in the hope that someone else can 'fix us'. They cannot.

As adults we can expand our ability to respond in relationships by viewing all negative experiences as opportunities for learning. This phase of your education may not truly begin until you leave formal schooling. The true path of perfect parenthood is perhaps one of pure *education* (*e-ducare*, the Latin root of the word meaning 'leading out from within') where all parties concerned draw deeply from their personal resources of loving, forgiveness and gratitude. It is a discipline, a positive choice, of learning to love all conditions equally.

Authentic Relationship

In entering into a new level of self-discipline, you are letting go of aspects of the old order which no longer serve you. This is much easier said than done. You may have inherited rules concerning how relationships 'should' be, and how you 'should' be within them. These unwritten rules tend to be etched into us unconsciously so that for the most part we are unaware of them.

The rules we have taken upon ourselves may have been those guidelines offered to us by our parents. We may have learnt from their example, or the example of other adults we observed. Some of the rules we may have made out of a reaction to our elders, choosing to do things in exactly the opposite way. We may have made our own rules for the sake of self-preservation.

If you saw your parents fighting, for example, you may have inwardly resolved never to get married because that is a destructive experience. If you once feared rejection or abandonment by a loved one, you might now have a rule about not allowing intimacy within relationships. Similarly, your loving sexual expression may be conditioned by limiting rules self-imposed as a result of old feelings of hurt, confusion and disappointment.

As you are now ready to expand, you can let go of self-destructive rules to become more of an authority **(I)** in your relationships with others **(O)**. You are now setting new, clear guidelines of kindness and compassion for yourself to increase your capacity for loving **(I)** + **(O)**. The goal is one of attaining 'authentic' relationships, where 'authentic' has the same root meaning as 'author' – and you are the author. Another way of stating this goal is you aim to become truer to yourself, where the 'self' concerned is not lonely, isolated and self-centred, but part of a larger picture, deeply connected with others both in your immediate, and more distant, worlds. As you write the guidelines **(I)**, you become less reactive to how others behave towards you.

Then, in authentic relationship, instead of reacting to the behaviour of others, you can increasingly observe and respond with loving awareness to any circumstance, thus becoming the cause and generator **(I)** of your experience in relationships **(O)**. This will not happen all at once. You may experience occasions when you need to admit to yourself that you are not 'emotionally equipped' to relate with certain people **(O)**, especially if you continually over-react **(I)** negatively towards them. If possible, you might choose to put those relationships on a back-burner until you are ready to resolve **(I)** your issues within them **(O)**.

Laying down new tracks of positivity, nurturing authenticity in your relationships with others, involves eliminating the negative and accentuating the positive. You cannot hope that the whole world will bow down and worship you for becoming more honest – in fact you may find yourself challenging in others the very issues you have healed in yourself. Some people may cease to be so important to you and no longer be part of your world. Relationships with those that remain, however, will be greatly enriched **(I)** + **(O)**.

Some guidelines for learning authentic relationship:

Take care of yourself **(I)**,
so that you can help take care of others **(O)**

Don't hurt yourself **(I)**,
and don't hurt others **(O)**

Use every opportunity to expand
your loving experience **(I)**
and expression of loving **(O)**

Choosing the Positive Option

It is not always easy to start making changes, even changes for the better. It may seem less trouble to stick with what you have got rather than risk the danger of trying something new and failing. So confronting entrenched emotional positions, attitudes, beliefs and behaviour may not happen until circumstances or events give you a shove.

Alternatively, you may have an inkling about a change you would like to effect, but on some level fear the consequences of addressing it.

In authentic relationship, *you* are making the choices and directing yourself in relationship to others. The positive option is:

Know yourself now.
Be true to yourself.

Sacrificing the Negative

Letting go of what you no longer want, whether that is a relationship, an attitude or pattern of behaviour, is often easier said than done. Until you can leave behind, or eliminate, what no longer serves you it becomes much more difficult to go for what you really want. But by undergoing some physical, mental and emotional housecleaning, you create a clear, fresh space for new experiences and greater fulfilment.

The best way to move physically away from a relationship, such as that with your parents when you leave home, or with a former spouse or close partner when you split up, is with a clean slate and an absence of bitterness, resentment or regret. When you are no longer in a position to generate healing experiences within a relationship, it is perhaps more important than ever to focus upon and recall only the *values* you received from once participating in it.

Concluding a relationship that has been close for you in the past calls upon you to find the way that first of all works best for you because, as much as you would like, you cannot save the other person from their own reactions, feelings or disappointment. Keeping a loving attitude alive **(I)** will enable as clean and as clear a break as possible **(O)**, and will honour the authentic relationship with yourself.

As we 'sacrifice the negative', we might even be *grateful* for the movement it has effected, whether that 'negative' came in the form of a person **(O)** with whom we experienced hurt or in the form of a limitation **(I)** (thought, belief, attitude or action) we held against our own capacity for loving (see *Growing from Grief to Gratitude*, page 113). Pain and suffering are often the cause of our being willing to make a change for the better. Not until we are fully sick and tired of being tired and sick do we finally choose to take some alternative action. In the overall pattern of our lives, even our negative experiences, hurt feelings and disappointments can be seen to serve us. Once you have sacrificed the negative, you can turn your attention to the positive. The following two exercises concentrate on this.

Laying Down the Positive Track

Once again, identify your 'expansion opportunity', that close challenging relationship in which you now wish to increase your experience and expression of loving. This would be a relationship in which you habitually experience or express a negative reaction towards the other person. This could be your mother, with whom you experience irritability when you are with her for more than half a day. It could be your son, who is aggressive and moody towards you. It could also be your spouse, whose habit of being the peacemaker was charming to you before you married, but has been infuriating since you started living together.

The trap of negative reactions is that you lose a sense of perspective, humour and creative choices of response. Becoming aware of the limitation is the first step to effecting a positive change and preferred choice.

The second step is to discharge the negative emotion by flooding your consciousness with the power of your loving. To do this, you will need to bring to mind a typical incident that causes the negative reaction within you. You might like to close your eyes for a moment to gather the details that surround your upset. For this to be effective, you need to put to one side any self-righteous indignation about the rights and wrongs of the issue.

Now bring to your mind whatever it is that triggers a loving response within you: a favourite animal, beautiful music, an ocean view, clear white light, your baby. Envisage that loving now filling you so completely that the negative emotion has no place inside you.

Glance once again at the scene of upset and notice how the negative charge has lessened, or possibly even totally gone. Switch into the loving once again and return to the former upset until all the negative emotion has been neutralized.

The discipline here is that of stopping your mind from entertaining doubts as to whether this technique will work. It has been said that the mind is a great servant, but a poor master. If you are not careful and caring, your mind may block you from creating the new possibilities that are now available to you.

Before you read on, take one relationship, or one typical reactive pattern you have in a challenging relationship, and do this exercise.

Learn to Say 'Stop'

As you commit to expanding, you can be more or less sure that inwardly you may experience forms of rebellion. Negative patterns may seem even more entrenched and reluctant to let go of their hold. Imagine telling a party of excitable schoolchildren that before they can go on a promised outing to a theme park, they have to take a series of maths tests! The strength of your positivity may be tested several times before you get to claim the reward you are seeking.

This exercise is easy to do, the most difficult aspect being actually remembering to do it. What it consists of is saying, as soon as you become aware of a negative thought:

'Stop!' or 'Stop that!'

Curiously perhaps, your mind will hear you and stop producing negativity, which is what you want. The relief you can then expect to experience from the absence of negative thinking is quite considerable. This exercise is surprisingly effective in producing a qualitative inner change.

As an experiment, the next time you are on your own, driving to work, going for a walk, in the house alone, for example, say, 'Stop!' several times aloud when your mind starts a negative pattern. With frequent practice, you will get better at stopping your negative thinking before your emotions become too destructive **(I)** + **(O)**. Without negative thinking, you will have space for laying down that new positive pattern of increased happiness and well-being in your relationship with yourself and others.

For the sake of testing this exercise, bring a challenging relationship to mind. Envisage the person concerned and observe your thinking. As soon as you become aware of a negative thought, say (out loud if possible):

'Stop that!'

until your mind leaves you alone. As a final move away from the negative pattern, think about something, or look at something near you, on which you can positively focus your attention.

Just imagine for a moment that negative thoughts are poison darts. As long as you are firing the poison darts of negative thinking, even unconsciously, towards another person, you cannot hope to expand your relationship **(I)** or **(O)**. If you were on the receiving end of someone else's poison darts, you might choose not to be very long in their company!

Simply learning to discipline yourself to sacrifice the negative will liberate you, and those around you, considerably.

Now let's turn to the third side of the *Triangle of Trust*.

3. Fun
Our capacity for humour is the saving grace in a dilemma. How much better it is for us if only we can laugh through our difficulties rather than indulge in self-pity. When put in perspective, the crises, dramas and tragedies enacted in our emotions are the stuff of high comedy – the moodiness of a troubled teenager, the affectionate foibles of elderly women, the 'will he, won't he/will she, won't she' dance of

courtship, the fights, or self-righteous non-communication, of marital disputes are all 'situation comedies' that can have us rolling in the aisles when they are not our own.

Appreciating our own emotionally upsetting experiences, however, may seem like a very tall order. To continually choose to love yourself, *and* those with whom you experience conflict **(I)** + **(O)**, is to win one of the greatest unseen battles. To say no to the negativity, and walk away from it if necessary, takes enormous courage and is a much tougher option than simply pointing the finger of blame.

But if we can only listen **(I)** to the message of loving that is being communicated through an upset **(O)**, we can come to realize how we are very blessed and have great cause for celebrating the many disguises in which loving expresses itself. Behind each dark rain cloud is the sparkle of warming sunshine. As we take steps to nurture the sparkle of delight within **(I)** we more easily perceive it in the events **(O)** that unfold around us. It is that delight that can lift us in the middle of our difficulties and assist us to endure with loving the challenges we meet. Our human spirit is highly resourceful in its capacities for creative loving.

Nurturing the Sparkle of Delight

This exercise can be done either to celebrate the conclusion of a period of conflict, **(I)** or **(O)**, or during a conflict to lift you into a higher perspective. In the latter case, it might be like calling a truce.

First of all, take a few moments and, with a pen and paper, reflect and note down what you most appreciate about yourself and anyone else concerned during a period of expansion and growth. This could be recent or far back. It is never too late to celebrate an unrecorded triumph. Notice particularly the gifts of loving that were expressed. Notice also those gifts of awareness that came in disguise. Even the negative expressions serve a positive purpose.

As you review and record your many blessings, **(I) + (O)**, become aware of a greater experience of fullness within you. Bring to mind one or more actions you can take to celebrate your loving, enjoyment and delight, either in honour of your loving towards yourself or the loving you share with one or more others. For example, you might meet, phone or write to someone to appreciate them for who they are. Make it something of an event – for example, if you meet, take a small gift like a flower, beautifully presented. If you phone, keep in mind – and in your voice – the warmth you have for them. If you write, choose a special card and let the message you write sparkle. There is no benefit in re-enacting any former misunderstanding – let that be a matter of the past and simply focus on the joy that is now present within you.

Your gift may be non-verbal, even anonymous. Send theatre tickets or flowers or a copy of a favourite book. If you are with the person and it is not possible to communicate verbally, you may hold a hand or share a hug, imagining your touch to be surrounded with a soft, pink loving light. One of the silent gifts that has been known to lift many a troubled consciousness is to repeat inwardly the following nine magic words:

'God bless you, I love you, peace, be still.'

If the word 'God' does not feel right for you, substitute whatever word would best represent loving, kindness or compassion for you.

Do not underestimate, or fail to celebrate, those inner struggles you have had to overcome, your personal trials to become more fully the loving person you truly are. Appreciate yourself for choosing the loving option when the choice was not obvious, for making the mistakes and being willing to learn from them, for enduring through the challenging times. Celebrate the loving that you are!

For example, if there was one exceptional challenge that you met, bring to mind the quality – courage, patience or understanding, for example – which enabled you to 'pass the test'. Give yourself a gift to honour that quality, such as a vase, a crystal or a plant, or write an inspirational poem, something that will possibly serve to remind you of that quality which is there for you if you ever need it in the future.

Doing this exercise will be like polishing the inner sparkle when it has become a little dulled by events. Not only will you bring the shine back into your own eyes **(I)**, but your willingness to shine can bring the sparkle back into the lives of others **(O)**.

Lighten your Load with Laughter

It has been shown that laughter assists the healing of negativity, whether that shows up mentally, emotionally or physically. You might consider making a special place in your home for humour, a cupboard, bookshelf, drawer, even a cardboard box. In it, you may put favourite comedy videos, cartoons, story books, jokes, personal anecdotes, photos of fun times. You could put photos of yourself and others laughing on a notice-board. Whatever will tickle you and stimulate the laughter response will be there for when you need it.

Expansion is Fun

To be consciously moving forward in your life, embracing the new opportunities as they offer themselves is richly rewarding. New opportunities arrive not only in the form of other people but in the naturally changing circumstances that happen to us all as we mature. Maturity, or even what is viewed as 'old age', need not be dull.

Emotional maturity may make for greater spontaneity, freedom and fun because we may have let go, and grown out, of some of the needs to conform, or react, to current conventional, acceptable actions or behaviour. We can perhaps dare to be more outrageous, to be more fully and naturally ourselves.

Keeping a Light Touch

To keep a light touch in your relationships, remember to include plenty of the following:

1. **Treats and rewards**
   . . . both for yourself **(I)** and your loved ones **(O)**. If you are waiting for someone else to give you what you want, go ahead and give it to yourself. You deserve to be good to yourself. When someone you care about is feeling down, surprise them with a kind observation. When you make the effort to improve a relationship, reward yourself, even if your attempt was not well-received by the other person. Sometimes, it may seem as if you can never please some people, so you may as well please yourself.

2. **Acknowledgments**
   Getting on well with yourself and others is not always easy. Give yourself full credit for every small effort you make towards your growth and expansion, whether that is within yourself **(I)** or in any other relationship **(O)**.

3. **Gratitude**
   In any negative condition, there is always a positive perspective for which to be grateful. If there is an absence of gratitude in your life, make the effort to rebuild it. For the next week, each morning set yourself the task of counting at least ten items in your life for which you are grateful – for example, warmth, electricity, a home, health, sanity, etc. – before you get up and begin the day.

We can heal much of our hurting when we can find a way to switch out of grief and into gratitude, as already discussed in the last chapter. As we learn how to relate with gratitude to others close to us, we are living the truest possible relationship with them. Also, when they are no longer with us, we have a residue of gratitude for who they were.

We can also feel gratitude for life itself. When we awaken to all of the opportunities being offered to us, we realize that life is a great gift.

Chapter 5

Rejoice

. . . It's a Wonderful Life

This chapter is dedicated to the Inner Child, the Inner Child in yourself and in those you love and actively care for.

Accepting the Value and Role of your Feelings

Early Trading and Negotiation

Remember that there is no 'path to perfect parenthood'. With the best will in the world, our parents were probably not psychic and did not, or could not, necessarily fulfil our every wish, heal our every hurt or cater for our every need, exactly as we wanted it and without our asking. So at an early age we learnt skills of trading and negotiation in relation to our wants.

For example, you might have been excited and looking forward for days to going to the circus (or football game or amusement park). Owing to adverse weather conditions, the circus was closed. To compensate for this loss, you were offered another treat, such as a toy. It was a trade, a compensation for what you really wanted. Even if you were not getting things just the way you wanted or anticipated, though, you were getting attention and establishing a connection, or relationship, with the resources of loving outside of yourself.

Denial of Feelings

It may be, however that your early relationship with outer loving resources was not an easy one. It is a rare parent who has the time and energy to accept and accommodate all the emotional ups and downs experienced and expressed by a growing child. How many of us can properly master our own emotional upheavals, far less those of anyone else, especially those for whom we care deeply?

All too often what we learnt as children was either how to evolve a strategy of denying that our feelings exist at all, or that we simply should not *value* our feelings.

Denial is a form of self-imposed 'loss' and loss produces in us a condition of grief. The loss of anything to which we are attached and have placed value, including our feelings, makes for an emptiness or sadness in our consciousness. Our feelings are extremely important to us because they are a source of guidance and inspiration for dealing with the world. If we lose attunement to our finer senses, then we may fail to receive either the benefits, or warnings, that the world around us may be giving us.

Have you ever been surprised **(I)** by the behaviour of someone **(O)** you thought you could trust? Have you ever found yourself doubting **(I)** your judgement in respect of people **(O)** you took on as partners or employees? Were you being given warning signs well in advance but failed to listen to them or chose to ignore them? Have you ever been disappointed **(I)** in the people around you, perhaps because you imposed your perception of them *on them* **(O)** rather than seeing them as they were, in relation to you?

The denial of our feelings may be further compounded if we have not only shut ourselves off from them, but also felt in some way bad about them, particularly about the so-called 'negative' ones. For example, feeling guilt, shame, jealousy, anger or even sexual attraction may have been considered 'bad', and therefore unacceptable, in your family, religious or cultural background. So, in order to be a lovable and acceptable member of your 'group' **(O)**, you may have chosen to bury those feelings **(I)** whenever they came close to surfacing in your experience of life. As a form of protection, you may have armoured yourself against the world to prevent discovery of these feelings you thought you should not be having.

If that has been your choice of strategy, it is a hard one to bear. You may well have experienced a lot of loneliness in your life so far, or sought various forms of compensation to fill in your *self-imposed* **(I)** emptiness. If you neglected the important sensory aspect of your life, you may have drawn towards you the kinds of people who also 'neglect' your feelings **(O)**, take advantage of, or in some way abuse you.

Self-imposed is the operative expression here. Although you may look back over your past and blame either yourself **(I)** or others **(O)** for the strategies you adopted for managing your life, given the information or knowledge you had at the time, you did the best you could with the material you had to hand. You need not, however, remain stuck with your former choices. If you imposed a certain restriction, then you can also remove it.

With the right encouragement and support, the Child within you has the creative resources you need to effect the freedom you would most like to enjoy. What is more, he or she is probably only too willing and eager to co-operate with you.

A Loving Reminder . . .

Before we explore some specific techniques and ideas for effecting the change of outlook and behaviour, here are a few suggestions to bear in mind:

1. **Patience**
   As already mentioned, the personal changes you wish will take whatever time they need. You may not be able to clearly anticipate the length of time required for each step. Also, you may need to take many steps before you finally arrive at your destination.

2. **Endurance**
   Do not give up too soon, before the process is fully complete for you. Prepare yourself as if you were going on a journey, even an adventure, of some indeterminate length. Know that you may cross some rough terrain **(I) + (O)** before you arrive.

3. **Loving**
   Be loving towards yourself **(I)** in your evolution. Love your mistakes, your false turns, even your old habits when they repeat themselves. Love the 'enemies' within you **(I)** and you will find they will gradually dissolve and fade from view, and those 'outside' you **(O)** will loosen, or lose, their hold over you.

4. **Support**
   See if you can identify at least one other person **(+ O)** that you can call on periodically to assist you to keep on track **(I)**. You do not have to disclose every working detail of your plan and progress, but you might find it very helpful to have someone who can give you encouragement when you feel discouraged or frustrated.

5. **Fun**
   The Inner Child loves to play. Did you play as much as you wanted when you were growing up? Did you ever get the impression that adult life was somehow a

burden? If you can make your plan of operation really enjoyable **(I)**, you will more easily secure the co-operation of your Child. Be prepared for some surprises and spontaneity along the way.

Imagination – It's Child's Play

The role of the imagination in adult loving relationships is often undervalued. We often take our issues and concerns far too seriously. It is common for us to 'go to sleep' on ourselves, shut off our self-awareness, not for the purpose of achieving rest, but as a form of distraction from our inner worlds of truth.

Children, though, have been known to see and do things that adults dismiss as 'impossible'. Given a safe and supportive environment, they will express just what is true for them in the moment. For this chapter, you might like to put to one side, lovingly, the sceptical adult side of your nature that could question, or doubt, that we live in a world of miracles and that dreams do indeed come true.

There may be many rungs of the ladder that you climb in order to attain your personal fulfilment. Each rung has its value for you. You may be someone who has undergone the physical challenges of firewalking, hang-gliding, mountaineering or bungee jumping to break through your crystallized fears and thinking. If these did not completely release you into the kind of inner freedom you seek, then they were perhaps just some of those steps on the way. If nothing else, you were at least moving. What is most important is knowing where you want the ladder to lead you. There may be many, many ways, possibly original and uniquely your own, that will enable you to get where you want to go. You can really have a lot of fun exploring, experimenting and discovering the limitless resources of your creative imagination.

Consider for a moment one or more areas in relationship with yourself **(I)**, or anyone else **(O)**, in which you feel stuck, inhibited, fearful or angry. You are going to be inviting your Inner Child to find some fun and imaginative ways that you can go beyond the obstacles you have imposed against yourself. You can begin by introducing a little magic into your life . . .

Create a Day of Magic

An important first part of this exercise is to consciously secure the co-operation of your Inner Child. This should not be difficult, but it is a formality that will bring you into alignment with the purpose of the exercise. You can do this as a dialogue with the Child, either mentally, if you have already established a good rapport, or on paper if you would prefer.

You might like to gently touch your stomach area around the navel to reassure and make a loving contact with your Child. If it feels good for you, you could imagine magic dust of light white particles flowing from your hands and surrounding the Child.

Begin the dialogue, however you would like. The example below shows how it might look:

Me: Good morning! How are you?
IC: Really good.
Me: Wonderful! Are you ready for some magic today?
IC: Yes. I thought you would never come to this bit.
Me: This is your chapter, you know.
IC: About time. I like the acknowledgment.
Me: I hope you will like the content even better. What we are going to be doing is creating a day of magic and I would like to have your assistance with this.
IC: We don't have to do anything dangerous, do we?
Me: Not if you don't want to. Would you like to have something of an adventure?

IC: OK.

Me: Here's the deal. I know that in the past I have placed all kinds of restrictions on what we can do, when we can do it and so on, all rules, rules, rules about behaving properly. On whose say so, I am not very sure. Most of them I think I have made up. I have gone a bit overboard with the discipline bit and I apologize for having squeezed out some of your vitality and fun in the process.

IC: OK, OK. What do you want me to do now?

Me: I'd like to break through the unnecessary rules.

IC: How am I supposed to know what is unnecessary from what is necessary?

Me: Good question. I think we are going to have to find that out – that is part of the adventure.

IC: Well, OK. But don't be angry with me if I break the wrong rules.

Me: Of course not. If we get into deep water – whatever that might be I am not sure, I suppose there could be flood warnings – anyway, what we do is imagine ourselves being sprinkled all over by those white particles of magic dust and we repeat the following statement, as often as necessary until the waters subside:

'I am forgiven.'

This is your magic statement for our day of magic together. Remember it at all times! I love you very much.

IC: That's another magic statement for me – remember it please.

Me: No problem.

IC: So what are we going to do on this day of magic?

Me: Glad you asked. It is not so much what we are going to do – in a way what we are doing is less important than

That our approach to whatever we are doing has a
quality of magic within it. How does that sound?

IC: No witches or broomsticks?

Me: Not exactly that kind of magic.

IC: I was just joking.

Me: You are getting the picture . . . Any questions?

IC: Not for now.

Me: Ready to go?

IC: When do we start?

Me: No time like the present, as the saying goes . . .

IC: You're on!

As here, you might simply have as a theme for your day that it is
one of magic for you. You could also apply your creativity in any way
you wish to produce experiences of magic, wonder and delight. For
example, if you chose to make an ordinary working day your day of
magic, then you might like to see your workplace and the people
within it through eyes of magic.

Look with fresh eyes for the unusual in your usual surroundings.
If the place seems a little dreary to you, then why not imagine
yourself sprinkling magic dust over your desk and papers? Scatter
it around someone if they are in a bad mood. Is there a problem that
seems difficult to resolve? Scatter magic dust all over it! You may
feel safer being discreet about this but you can still smile inwardly.
Look at every event and happening with the eyes of delight.

Have you ever noticed how children seem to be motivated to bring
joy into our lives and to break through the crystallized thinking of
our adult selves? You can now allow the Child within you to bring
more joy into your everyday life.

If you have some extraordinary experiences with this exercise –
and they could well happen – you might like to make a note in a
journal so that when you need the reminder in future, you can read
about your resources of personal magic.

Reclaiming the Dream

Did you, in the course of growing up, lose your capacity for dreaming? Not the kind of dreams you have at night but those of your waking heart. Did you ever imagine yourself as a ballet dancer? A star footballer? An Olympic gold medallist? A rock drummer? A film star, dressed in glamorous clothes, rich and richly admired? Or did you perhaps take on life's realities as difficulties to be suffered?

You may be someone who is reluctant to dream in case the dream does not come true. This could be especially true in the area of relationships **(I) + (O)**. Former hurts may have temporarily shut some of your doors of opportunity. The good news is that as you awaken your capacities for loving yourself **(I)**, and gradually extend that loving into your relationships **(O)**, you are realigning yourself with yet more of your positive attributes, the function of dreaming being just one.

What, you may be asking yourself, has having dreams got to do with improving your personal relationships? Dreams **(I)** play a vital part in freeing yourself from the often buried rules you may be holding about the ways successful relationships **(O)** work. Your dreams may simply be buried until such time as you are ready to receive and realize them. That time could well be now.

It may seem strange, but dreaming itself is sometimes more important than actually fulfilling your dreams in every last detail. This is not to deny the dream. Far from it. It is more a question of setting priorities in your thinking. Occasionally, we may try to control our destiny with too limited a vision. Keep closely in your mind those *qualities* you most want to experience in your life. Allow yourself some flexibility **(I)** and room to manoeuvre in generating the relationships **(O)** that enable you to have those qualities more vibrantly within you. You could become disappointed when expectations in the outer world do not get fulfilled.

But if you keep an open mind, your creative resources are free to supply your dreams in outer forms that you might never have considered. Perhaps the main value of our dreams is in giving us a sense of direction **(O)**, which will lead us to the inner experiences **(I)** we most want to have.

What may seem like a very radical approach, but one that can work, is to envisage **(I)** the very best relationship **(O)** you would like to have, no matter with whom – a romantic partner, a new baby, a close friend or a working colleague. It might be a new relationship or a greatly improved existing relationship. You will need to suspend all your disappointments, frustrations and irritations concerning previous experiences, and have a basic foundation of loving detachment towards yourself **(I)** and the other person **(O)**. Deep down you can formulate your relationship dream.

This is an intuitive activity **(I)** in which your Inner Child will be assisting and inspiring you. A sense of wonder, fun and attunement with the delight of your Inner Child is the most fertile mental ground **(I)** for profound inner growth and expansion in your relationship **(O)** dreams. In advance, you might like to agree a reward that you will give to yourself (the Child within) on completion of this exercise. You can also let him or her know that you will not be taking any action without practically evaluating its feasibility. Your Child may feel reassured to know that there is a co-operative adult around, able to respond authentically in new circumstances.

Dreaming the Dream

Have you been sitting around, mentally at least, moaning and groaning either about the lack of the perfect relationship in your life or about the lacks in a current relationship? Then do this exercise now and prepare to have lots of fun with it.

Before you begin, decide what reward you will be giving to

yourself (as the Inner Child) once you have completed the exercise.

This exercise could be divided into two stages: first of all, the part that follows here; secondly, following through with any action that you wish to take as a result of the exercise.

Begin by reflecting inwardly with the following guided visualization. As before, you could simply read through it here, pausing to look within periodically, or you could record it on cassette to listen to in full with your eyes closed, or you could have someone read it out to you. In any case, ensure that you will be undisturbed.

Take in a few deep breaths . . . Relax . . . Become aware of your Inner Child . . . Let him/her know that you will be spending some time together . . . time to play and have fun . . . Whatever ideas you come up with together are just fine . . . There is no criticism . . . no censorship . . .

This will be free time . . . Time to dream . . . In this dream . . . whatever you want can be yours . . . All the loving you have ever longed for can come to you . . . You do not have to put up with less than you really want . . . You are living in a world rich with gifts of love . . . Reach out and you will receive . . .

What is it you would now most like to receive? Is it appreciation . . . tenderness . . . affection . . . intimacy with someone you trust . . . the strength of someone you know is truly there for you . . . kindness . . . acts of consideration and thoughtfulness . . . generosity being extended towards you . . . freedom to express yourself to someone who is accepting and uncritical towards you . . . acceptance of who you are . . . space to feel your vulnerability . . . to feel emotional . . . safe . . . with a loving understanding heart . . .

What is most important for you to receive? Allow yourself to reach out and receive those gifts that are now available for you . . . Envisage them coming towards you and let the giver of them remain unidentified . . . This time is just for you to receive your heart's desires . . . You just have to know what they are . . .

Experience the fullness within you now as you envisage yourself receiving the gifts that are coming to you . . . Feel a sense of

gratitude as you receive . . . Keep clearly in mind what those gifts
are as you bring your attention back into the world immediately
around you . . .

Take a sheet of paper. Draw a circle in the middle, or a heart shape
if you prefer, and 'map' out those gifts. If more come to mind as
you do this, add them in. This is a game of expansion, not limitation.
Figure 10 illustrates how this might look.

The exercise may be complete for you now, in which case reward
yourself as agreed. If this is not convenient right now, set a time
when you will and make sure you fulfil this commitment. It is
important for ensuring the further co-operation of your Inner Child.

An option with this exercise is to 'anchor' this experience
into your body. Anchoring is a technique to reinforce your
internal imagery so that you can translate your vision more
easily into working reality. An anchor is a physical touch,
such as rubbing an earlobe, holding a thumb and forefinger
together or touching an elbow.

Many of us have mannerisms of some kind, of which we
are unaware for the most part. Have you ever noticed
people who pull at their chin, for example, when they feel
shy? There is often an unconscious connection between
such mannerisms and the internal make-up. The person
who is feeling uncomfortable inside (I) will 'communicate'
the discomfort (O) beyond superficial appearances.

By using powerful creative imagery and an anchor you
can positively enhance the experience (I) of your dream and
give yourself the confidence to communicate (O) it both
consciously and unconsciously to others. To give you an
idea of how your creative imagination makes an impact on
your inner environment, imagine sucking on a lemon and
notice how your body responds. Can you imagine the scent
of a rose on a warm summer day? Bring to mind the love
you have for your child, a dear friend, your spouse or lover
and notice how that feels inside. What is the most beautiful

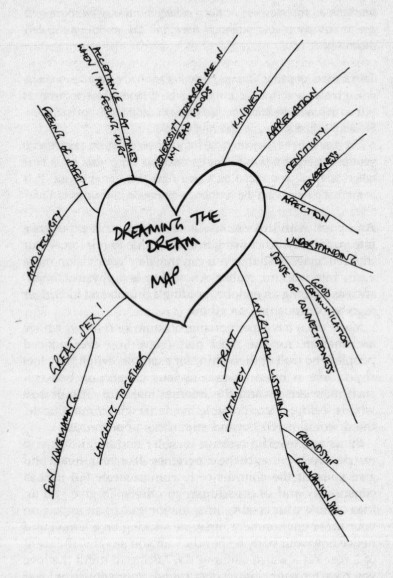

Figure 10: 'Dreaming the dream' map.

scene you can bring to mind – a sunset, a huge expanse of green countryside, sunrise over a lake, snow-capped mountain peaks? Now think of a sound, the sound of an ocean, for example, or a waterfall, the breeze in leafy trees. Certain images that you can envisage with all of your senses will give you a powerful, positive emotional experience.

It is when you have a peak moment of this experience inwardly that you can create your physical 'anchor' as a reference point. In future, this anchor of peak emotional experience will serve to revitalize you with the powerful positive qualities of your dream. Your anchor should be something you can easily do without drawing attention towards yourself. It is like a secret contact you are making with your creative Inner Child as a reinforcement of your dream. This could be more effective by keeping the action a secret between you and your Child.

You might like to choose now the anchor that will work best for you. Then review the visualization and the dream map, experiencing as fully as possible the gifts as you receive them. At the point of greatest inner fullness, touch your anchor. You could do this two or three times.

Then over the next week, or whatever period of time you decide, retouch your anchor at least once a day. At the conclusion of this second period of time, give yourself that reward you promised. Remember that it is important to follow through on these commitments to reward yourself.

Allow plenty of time for the results to show up, maybe even a year or more. In the meantime, keep breathing your dream, let it literally 'inspire' you, and remember that miracles do not necessarily happen overnight.

Guardian Angels of your Growth (Listeners)

Perhaps one of the hardest things for us as adults to realize is that we are not always in full control of ourselves **(I)** or others **(O)**, in the way we would like. You may, of course, be someone who naturally embraces a considerable degree of chaos in your life, flowing along with things as they happen. Alternatively, you may be happier anticipating that certain actions will inevitably result in clearly definable outcomes.

Knowing what you want **(I)**, you can allow an element of creative chaos, serendipity or spontaneity in producing it. Another way of looking at this would be to see it as a high level of co-operation coming from the happy integration **(I)** of your rational and imaginative inner resources. This state of harmonious vitality comes as a result of the inner attunement with yourself, being true to and honouring your inner guidance **(I)**, even when this seems at odds with others **(O)** around you.

You may be someone who has had cause to feel the presence **(O)** of a 'Guardian Angel'. At a time of crisis, you could have experienced life events turning in such a way to your advantage that it was as though some divine presence stepped in and saved the day. There may, of course, also been times when you would have wished for such deliverance! It seems that we almost need to stumble and graze our knees once in a while. If nothing else, it may keep us humble.

Perhaps it is true that Guardian Angels will not prevent us from learning the necessary lessons that hardship may provide. What is extraordinary is how, during times of hardship or deprivation, we may make a first contact with an indefinable benevolence around us, despite the conditions we may have to endure. Astronauts, prisoners of war and former hostages, having survived terms of isolation, have reported awakening to a greater sense of meaning in life **(I)** through their experiences of solitary challenges and adversity.

Whether or not you have so far enjoyed the benevolence of a Guardian Angel – or the admiration of grandparents or the fun and friendship of aunts or uncles **(O)** – you can now, if you wish, select and appoint **(I)** a caring adult figure for your Inner Child. Specifically, this could be a friend to whom the Child within you could speak his/her mind without fear of criticism, knowing that whatever you are experiencing **(I)** this person will offer love **(O)** and reassurance, even guidance or assistance. Any exercises you have been doing to establish trust and confidence with your Inspirational Self **(I)** will assist you in attracting the trust and confidence of one or more others **(O)** who *will* love and support you. The inner work that we do to nurture ourselves enables us to become better receivers from those around us.

You might not be able to think of anyone immediately that would fit the bill. But once you can envisage **(I)** the part a caring figure could play in your life, and you in his or hers **(O)**, you will be amazed how that person will appear in your life as though they were just waiting for your 'call'.

This next exercise will assist you as you allow yourself contact with the Inner Child in creating a role **(O)** for your *Fairy Godparent*. To work this exercise successfully, you will need to put aside your adult considerations, or reservations, about fairies, God (or gods) and parents, even ineffective godparents, if you had any. Are you ready to play? Now is the time . . .

Preparing a Fairy Godparent Charter

Did you know that the world is full of people who quietly enjoy extraordinary events that they have come to accept as normal, but which possibly for you, would be remarkable, if not 'miraculous'? These might be the wise ones who embrace life itself as the miracle that it is. They may have their share of difficulties, but they have seen and know that there is more to life than meets our physical eyes.

This is the sort of person you might wish to meet and appoint as your Fairy Godparent. The inner appointment **(I)** is the significant one. You may or may not wish to formally let your Godparent know the nature of his or her role in your life. Your Fairy Godparent could be in any walk of life, so be slow in either dismissing, or appointing, the potential Fairy Godparent. You might wish to be careful about expecting more from him or her than is possible. As with many relationships, it is often a matter of 'horses for courses'.

Fairy Godparents are especially helpful in those circumstances which seem unresolvable. Your Child needs to feel that he/she can reach up a hand and know that it will be met by the equivalent of a firm and reassuring grasp. Your Inspirational Self can sometimes provide this, but the Fairy Godparent is another potentially valuable resource. Your Fairy Godparent might be the torch bearer who holds the warmth and light of encouragement as you move forward, learn and grow. The encouragement he/she gives to you could be in the forms of a phone call, time to be together to talk, letters written, hugs shared.

Consider once more a current 'sticky' relationship in your life. There must be many other people, not necessarily in your immediate environment right now, who have encountered similar obstacles. A local bookshop or library could well have catalogued books addressing your particular issue. We are never completely alone in what we feel.

Your Fairy Godparent could be someone who has already gone through and learnt from an experience similar to yours, or who may have learnt from the example of someone else or may just have the wisdom to know what to say to give you what you need at any one time. Recognize also that you, as the Fairy Godchild, may have gifts to bring your Godparent. You may have occasion to discover that the boot is on the other foot. Godparenting is a two-way street, and has little to do with age as such.

As with any relationship, the agreements you make within yourself or expectations you hold towards any other person need to be very clear and workable. The charter that you draw up could look something like the one that follows or be very different. You may wish to appoint your Godparent silently within yourself **(I)**, or notify him/her so that he/she is consciously **(O)** aware of his/her role in your life. Err on the side of caution when it comes to specific agreements or expectations, keeping them as open as possible for creativity, innovation, spontaneity and flexibility.

The Realm of Magic and Surprises

A significant part of the Fairy Godparent Charter given in the example is that of Magic and Surprises. Would you recognize a Magic and Surprise, if you could have one? It is an important part of the joy and celebration of life. When you grew up, did you have parties to celebrate your birthday each year? Did you get taken out for special treats when there was no particular occasion to celebrate? Did you have clothes for special occasions? Were you ever made to feel special for just who you are?

You may have said 'yes' to all of those questions, in which case you may have some happy memories stored as part of your personal enrichment. If, however, you experienced any sadness or lack in that area of your childhood you may dismiss Magic and Surprises as being unimportant for you. After all, you have survived very well to date. Who needs Magic and Surprises anyway?

You may have been educated and raised in the hard school of endurance and survival. Many of us were. But, as you now know, the past need not necessarily continue

FAIRY GODPARENT CHARTER

_____ as Fairy Godfather/mother

and

_____ as Fairy Godson/daughter

undertake to

have fun together

write letters

see each other when we can

always have hugs

and most importantly
they actively promote
Magic and Surprises

when either of them have any issues,
these can be aired and discussed
and

Magic and Surprises
be brought in to resolve them.

into your future. As we learn to switch our thoughts up (see the exercise *Switch Up*, pages 66–7), our feelings follow and we feel lifted. As we lift up, we reach into a level where Magic and Surprises are the natural order.

So many of us have yet to grow out of the childhood limitations and expectations of our powerlessness in relation to those to whom we have given authority over our lives **(I) + (O)**, consciously or otherwise. Whether or not you had all the joy you wanted as a child growing up, you can change the emphasis of your life now to invite more joy as a pervading theme throughout your daily endeavours.

Have you ever noticed how children have a short attention span? They can often move rapidly from one activity, or point of absorption, to another. In effect, what they are doing is moving from one choice to the next choice. They will naturally move towards an activity that gives them pleasure and away from one which causes pain. Children are also endowed with the ability to pretend, to imagine the extraordinary within very ordinary resources. Now, as an adult, encountering what appear to be limitations within a relationship, you can draw on that same imagination. The role of Magic and Surprises in our adult lives is to recapture the kind of immersion where, just for perhaps a short time, we are lifted above the ordinary in our lives and reach into the extraordinary.

You can recognize the power your loving has to lift both yourself and another person who is important to you to a new level of experience **(I)** in your relationship. As an independent witness, you can soar like an eagle above any difficulty and, out of ear-shot, observe the humour in less-than-loving interactions. In your mind, you can exaggerate the motions you observe and watch them transform, in slow-motion, to become endearing, powerful, pro-active or however you wish them to become.

Challenges within close relationships are seldom one-sided. When you can lift yourself above the challenge level, and rise into the realm of Magic and Surprises, you enter into the field of infinite resource where anything is possible.

As you open to the many opportunities for Magic and Surprises to happen within your relationships, they will arrive, sometimes when you least expect them, or at the point when you thought you had run out of ideas. You can positively expect the unexpected to deliver you a gem! Try the next exercise, in which you have the freedom to honour and celebrate the special essence within you **(I)** in a specific way, letting an overflow of your enjoyment extend **(O)** to one or more others.

Treatfeast

We are sometimes taught that if we see ourselves as special, then we set ourselves apart from others. This need not be so. If you truly recognize the special within yourself **(I)**, you may more easily perceive that which is special within others **(O)**.

In this exercise, let the joy within you determine a treat, special outing, event or occasion and, as you do so, intuitively identify the relationship(s) you can enrich, the person, or people, with whom you can best fulfil your treat.

There is a subtle distinction here between serving others whom you recognize as being in some capacity 'needy' and allowing your own personal experience of pleasure to radiate easily, touching and igniting the spark of pleasure within others. The former can become stressful or a burden after a while because it may be one-sided giving; the latter demands that you first maintain your own levels of well-being so that your giving is truly unconditional.

This exercise is one which you will be undertaking out in the world. Whether or not you are currently leading a busy and full life, allocate a clear chunk of time for planning, preparation and then enjoying the treat.

There are four steps to this exercise:

1. Make your clear choice of treat. Let your imagination run free and think of some of the impossible treats you might like before you select one, or more if you wish. Below are some suggestions:

   a day at a theme park

   an evening at a jazz club

   an elegant dinner/dance for two

   a swim with a dolphin

   a Magical Mystery Tour with your spouse

   a walk through an area of exceptional scenic beauty

   a day of delight with your darling parent/child/partner

   a trip to the circus, zoo, art gallery, museum, theatre

   a night in a luxury hotel

   a tap dancing/singing/yoga/painting/drumming lesson

2. Do whatever it is you need to do in order to bring about your treat, including inviting the one or more others to share it with you. There are a few points to consider here:

   Do you need to make special arrangements in order to have the time available?

   Do you need any outside assistance in bringing about your treat?

   Are there any inner obstacles to overcome in order to enjoy your treat to the full?

   How can you plan your treat so as to fully celebrate the special essence that you are?

   Are there any finishing touches that you need to think about in your planning and preparation?

3. Receive your treat

   As you receive your treat to the full, be aware of the extraordinary that happens for you . . . Allow for the unexpected . . . See the humour in however your treat unfolds for you . . . What do you become aware of in yourself, or anyone else, through this experience . . .?

4. Celebrate the gift of life **(I) + (O)**

   Retain something of your treat to serve to remind you of the gift that you are. It might be a photograph, a single word or phrase, a joke.

Waking the Sleeping Giant of Intuition

As your sense of authenticity, or integrity, expands, you will
awaken to more of the resources and gifts that are presently
latent within you. Receiving these gifts **(I)** is mainly a
matter of being aware of them. As we awaken to our gifts
and utilize them in service to ourselves **(I)** and others **(O)**,
there is cause for great rejoicing.

One of these gifts is that of your intuition. You may
increasingly trust your intuition as a 'feeling', a 'still, small
voice' or a set of 'visual cues' which guides you out of
unnecessary conflicts and towards those circumstances
which enhance your life **(I)**, and as a consequence those
with whom you relate **(O)**. Promoting healing within our
relationships, **(I) + (O)**, is often like crossing unknown
territory in the dark, so intuitive guidance can be very
useful.

To effect constructive changes in your relationships **(O)**,
you need to be sensitive **(I)** to appropriate timing for taking
action. 'Everything in its season', as they say, and you need
to recognize those times when it is more productive to hold
steady, waiting until, inwardly, you get the go ahead to
make an outer move.

Through our intuition, we may touch into the essential
'divine connectedness' between ourselves and others. You
may have answered the phone and found yourself speaking
to a friend you had just been thinking about. It is possible
to establish a clear connection to what might be termed the
'spiritual' source of your being and from there 'tune in' to
others. Even when other forms of communication have
failed, or are not available, you can always make an inner
contact and express loving to a person who is out of reach.

What if we preselected our relationships **(O)** *to learn* to
love all experiences **(I)** unconditionally? Look with new
eyes to the circumstances that your life is currently placing
at your feet. How can you now embrace with a grateful

heart each opportunity, or blessing, no matter how well disguised, to learn **(I)**, give **(O)** and grow **(I)**?

Trust your intuition, for it will both guide you towards your next lessons and take you through them to completion. The course of learning itself is a gift because it touches those qualities you have yet to awaken **(I)** within yourself. Then, perhaps paradoxically, as you give of your gifts to others **(O)**, you fully receive them **(I)**.

It may take a quiet mind to appreciate the steady, progressive deliverance from your issues and upsets, but you have access to this if you choose to be aware of it. In this next exercise, you can take yourself to that higher level of appreciation at which you can see more clearly some of the gifts being brought to you.

Entertaining the Divine within You

What did you come to learn **(I)** in your relationships **(O)**? How can you increase the enjoyment of your education? Is there any part of your consciousness that particularly needs healing? How can you release any feelings of separation **(I)** and restore the true divine connectedness between yourself and others **(O)**?

A very good starting-point is that of an open mind, a state of what might be described as 'not knowing'. Life truly is a gift that unfolds, wrapper by wrapper. You may glimpse occasionally the most precious essence deeply within the gift wrapping.

Imagine for a moment your life now as a gift-wrapped package. Your current frame of mind might determine the quality of wrapping. Do not be dismayed if your package looks like an overused, crumpled brown paper bag. Sometimes the greatest of gifts are concealed in the most deceptive of coverings.

Whatever the wrapping – ribbon, bows, string, sealing wax, rubber bands, balloons, flowers, a tin trunk, paper, plastic, tree bark, palm fronds, a glass bowl, silk, foam polystyrene – allow it to form in your mind. You might like to sketch it, as in Figure 11. As with all the drawing exercises, do not be concerned if artistic expression is not your strong suit.

Figure 11: Gift-wrapping.

Remember, the wrapping may give you no clue whatsoever as to the *contents* of your package. The wrapping is in itself a 'gift of learning'. As you receive the learning, symbolically represented by the wrapping, you will begin to discover your greater gifts contained within it.

The wrapping indicates to you three current areas of your learning, so now complete each of the following sentences at least once. Whatever pops into mind spontaneously, write down. Allow the Child within you to respond with whatever is true for him/her now.

♥ I am learning to love . . .
♥ I am learning to value . . .
♥ I am learning to appreciate . . .

This part of the exercise might look something like this:

♥ I am learning to love different personalities.
♥ I am learning to value my friends.
♥ I am learning to appreciate the courage in my boss.
♥ I am learning to appreciate my tenderness.
♥ I am learning to love my auntie.
♥ I am learning to value my sense of purpose.

Now take one each of the most important love, value and appreciate statements and set them aside to read through as an affirmation (see pages 30–3) before going to sleep tonight. When you wake up, make a note of any insights that come to mind about these areas of learning and see if there is some way you can actively demonstrate **(I)** or **(O)** that the learning has taken place. When you can observe a change of behaviour **(O)**, then you will know that the learning **(I)** is complete.

For example:

♥ I am learning to love different personalities.
    I demonstrate patience and a sense of humour towards my mother-in-law when she sniffs imperiously in order to get my attention.

♥ I am learning to value my friends.
    I demonstrate by communicating to them how they are important for me.
♥ I am learning to appreciate the courage in my boss.
    I demonstrate my appreciation of his employing me when I was not the most qualified candidate and potentially a risk to the business.

Your Cosmic Joke
To return to your gift-wrapped package, if the layers of wrapping are the learning, what is the gift contained within it? The gift on this occasion might best be described as a cosmic joke.

What symbolically is the cosmic joke that will remind you to keep looking for the funny side? It might be a crystal that sparkles, a banana skin, a catch-phrase that somehow tickles you, a vessel to contain your laughter, a ditty to distract you, a dance in your heart.

Without thinking about it too much, draw your cosmic joke. Then in a sentence or two, describe it and how it serves to entertain the divine in you and others. Figure 12 illustrates how a cosmic joke might look.

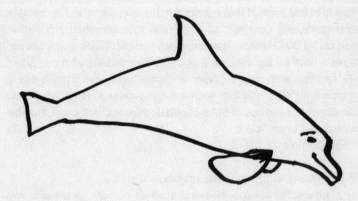

Figure 12: My cosmic joke is a dolphin because he always looks so happy and carries a smile on his face. I give this gift to others when I see how funny life is and communicate a humorous point of view when we all seem to be taking life too seriously.

How can we more completely *share* the cosmic joke, entertain the divine, receive the tuition we came to gain? The answer is to keep looking for the funny side. It is a matter of attunement **(I)**, of intuition, of seeing, in the middle of doubt, despair or disappointment, the quietly radiating sparkle of wisdom and humour.

Acts of Loving (I) + (O)

If, deep down, you still doubt that you are loved, that you are love, acts of loving **(O)** + **(I)** will transcend and transform those doubts.

Acts of loving are really a simple way out of our dilemmas. What counts is not quantity here, but quality. A small act of thoughtfulness **(O)** can move mountains, inwardly and outwardly. In time, these small acts **(O)** build as a mountain of loving **(I)** in your consciousness.

Expand outwards **(O)** with a loving heart **(I)** and do not be put off by any monsters you fear may be lurking at the gates of your awareness. Try dressing in the protective clothing of your greatest loving qualities before venturing forth.

Your Garment of Invincible Clothing

Imagine that your Garment of Invincible Clothing has nine facets to it. You can imagine dressing yourself in each facet, holding each to you with a bonding of clear white light. Each facet is like a prayer from your Inner Child.

The facets are such qualities as:

loving
caring
sharing
humour
gratitude
happiness
abundance
enthusiasm
forgiveness

You could adopt these, or choose any that you feel would best arm you.

As you may be aware, fashion these days can take many forms. For example, you might envisage a Sunhat of Abundance, A Cloak of Happiness, a Shirt of Gratitude, Gloves of Sharing, Trousers of Enthusiasm, Socks of Caring, Shoes of Forgiveness, a Belt of Loving, Underwear of Humour . . . Alternatively, you could simply envisage a huge garment with each of the prayers sewn together with white thread as panels. Yours might be a marathon-run training outfit, a ballgown or a space suit. Imagine you are a fashion designer, and 'sketch' your Garment if that would help you to envisage it (Figure 13 is an example).

Your Invincible Clothing can be any design that you wish, any material, real or imaginary, the colour that best matches your prayers. Allow your Child now to dress you in the protective clothing. Your Garment of Invincible Clothing will protect you, whoever you encounter. As you wear it, you become a walking prayer that is constantly nurtured.

To complete this exercise, enter your inner worlds and imagine yourself clothed in those special qualities as you communicate with someone you might have identified as a 'petty tyrant'. Those qualities will offer no resistance to your 'foes', no reason for them to attack or harm you. More than that, they will enable a bridge to be made between the loving quality within you **(I)** and the loving quality within the other person **(O)**. When you meet for real, your

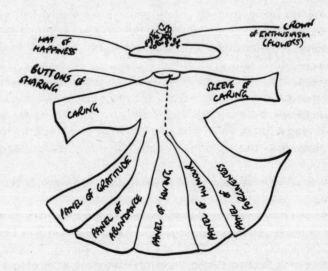

Figure 13: The Garment of Invincible Clothing.

garment will enable you to maintain the flow of loving from within you, out to the other person. You will know that you have contributed at 100 per cent of your capacity. (Remember, you are not responsible for how your loving communications are received.)

Set the Children Free!

This chapter was dedicated to the Inner Child. At the end of each day, we may talk to our (outer) children to hear how their day went for them, what they enjoyed, what went well, what they did not like about the day, what went less than well. Listening to our children in this way assists them to close their day with a peaceful mind and an open heart, having had the chance to talk about those things that mattered to them, and then benefit from a good night's rest. This daily loving contact forges the bond that makes for secure and trusting relationships into the teen and adult years.

As you bring yourself into greater inner alignment, you may also take a few moments before sleeping to listen, comfort, congratulate, forgive and reassure yourself, as the Child within you. The more we can daily complete, by healing, those inner differences of the day, the less 'work' we may have to do as we sleep, unconsciously resolving our difficulties. By resting at night with as quiet a mind, and as loving a heart, as we can give ourselves, we become free to soar into the possible dreams of our greatest loving potential.

Chapter 6

Love

. . . Life in All its Forms

It has been said that enough loving heals all things. In issues concerning our personal relationships, love, or loving, is the answer to most of our questions.

In this chapter, we shall be reviewing in the light of our loving the themes explored in the previous chapters. There may be times when remembering to choose a loving approach takes an enormous step of courage and honesty, but your inner resources can provide you with any insights and strength you need.

The loving within you is your primary resource to transform your inner world from doubt, fear or anger to confidence, freedom and enjoyment. In working through some of the exercises – or even reading through them – in the last chapter, you may have found yourself experiencing your Inner Child both in the child*like* state of purity, innocence, observation and acceptance and in the child*ish* state of emotional hurt, 'separation', jealousy or resentment. There seems to be a fine line between the two attitudes or conditions of mind. The child*like* state in you may have prompted the child*ish* to read *Superlove*.

The childlike state is one of openness, trusting, ease and grace, which leads to our happiness. The childish one is that human side of ourselves which we encounter and indulge, even unconsciously, from time to time. We all too easily fall into the habitual patterns of emotionally reacting, either against others **(O)**, or, often more subtly, against ourselves **(I)**. Indulging negative emotions towards anyone, including yourself, will ultimately hurt you the most.

This is because we are not honest about what it is we really want: *loving*. When we fall into the pattern of negatively trying to 'score points' in a relationship, we lose sight of both the loving within ourselves and our 'opponent', the net result being loneliness, isolation and a sense of inner separation. When these kinds of condition show up in your relationships, look with the eyes of loving to bring the healing into yourself **(I)**, so that you can once again extend loving towards others **(O)**.

What if you were able to view all of your relationships with the eyes of loving and appreciation? It may seem like a tall order, but supposing you could see the loving intention behind even the most negative of circumstances. You might not necessarily be able to cure all the relationship imbalances you see happening in the world, but you will at least be in a better position to address any disturbances you experience within the relationships that concern you directly.

If you have felt reluctant to do any of the exercises so far, you may find the simple ones that follow an easier start in creating greater happiness in your relationships. A little loving can go a very long way, but the journey begins with yourself. You must make the first move, so make it easy on yourself to take that step, however small. Minor adjustments can sometimes make an enormous impact.

Superloving begins with . . .

Self-Acceptance . . .
The Relationship with Yourself (I)

The symbol of Jesus being born in a stable is perhaps a reminder to us that we are first and foremost human, and perhaps vulnerable. No matter how ordinary, insignificant

and unpromising our entry, we nevertheless embody the
life-sustaining resources of loving to lift the awareness of
our lives above our human state.

When we are feeling upset, we often lose sight of that
which we want and need the most: *to be loved*. Not only
that, but in our unhappiness, we shut off, like a valve, our
capacity for restoring happiness. As a result of this self-
rejection, we also forget that we are essentially loving and
worthwhile people. Our self-esteem tumbles.

The first, and on some occasions the hardest, step to take
in improving the quality of any of your relationships is to
accept that you are a loving person; to accept that your true
motivation is to express and experience loving. If you are
not experiencing all the happiness you would like, the
chances are that you have lost contact with your innermost
source of love.

To accept once again your essential goodness **(I)**, the
following exercise will assist you in observing the
smokescreen that may be obscuring your view. Do not be
concerned about 'how' the smokescreen might have
formed in the first place, or 'who' put it there. All you know
is that it is there and that you are now going to examine it
and take a peek behind it.

Loving Observation – The Key to the Door of your Happiness

For this brief exercise, you will be assuming that every aspect of
yourself that you may encounter has a positive purpose. Any
smokescreen that stands in the way of your loving is there for a
reason, but right now we are not looking for any reasons. The task
is simply one of observing without asking any questions or venturing
any opinions about it, one way or another.

Successfully observing, releasing the pressure of needing to know about everything that may be going on, will enable you to relax and ease the tensions associated with any emotional upset. Give yourself just five to ten minutes to practise this relaxation exercise.

Begin by taking in a few really deep breaths. As you breathe out, let go of any tensions. Particularly, let you shoulders drop down, as it is often in the shoulders that we store tension. Make sure you are sitting or lying down in such a way that your body is comfortable and well supported. Loosen any clothing that feels tight.

All you are going to be doing is observing. First observe your physical body. Notice any places of tightness and tension. Do not do anything about them. Just look at them. Let your attention move up gradually from your toes to the top of your head, remembering also your arms and hands. It is through your hands that you reach out to others, to give and receive loving.

Next, notice any emotions that you are feeling. They may even be associated with certain parts of your body. You may become aware of happy feelings, sad feelings or anything in between. Again, do not do anything with these observations. Just watch your feelings, as though you were looking at the coloured patterns of a kaleidoscope.

Then, observe your thinking. When we are anxious, our thoughts can race. Now just observe them. Imagine that they are clouds passing across a clear blue sky on a warm, sunny, summer's day. You do not need to chase them, or feel pursued by them. Look at their shapes and sizes, the intensity of their colour. Some may be light and fluffy-looking, others may seem dark and foreboding. They are just clouds, so let them pass.

Take in a few more deep breaths and, this time, become aware of your heartbeat. The heart is a reminder to you of your loving, of the energy that constantly sustains you throughout all of your relationships. Other people may come and go in your life: your heartbeat, and the loving it represents, remains with you constantly.

As you learn to become a more skilled observer, you take into your own hands the key to open the door to your happiness. In this more relaxed frame of mind, you can once again get in touch with and accept the loving within you. Even if only for a moment, you can re-enter a state of inner calm and happiness. It is always there for you. Here and now, you can begin to see with fresh eyes the new options available to you. From your own centre of well-being and fulfilment, you can more fully appreciate others **(O)**.

Understanding . . . Personal Accountability and Co-operation

The approach to understanding in relationships being offered here is based upon your intuition, of clearly knowing inwardly what is true for you. In an unhappy state, we often react against our better judgement, so positive thinking alone may fail to produce the solution to the problem as we experience it. The sensitivity that enables us to feel pain, and seek understanding, is the same sensitivity with which we can experience pleasure, fulfilment and meaning in our lives.

Emotional discomfort can be a form of awakening and recognizing qualities in you that so far have been dormant. Relocation, divorce or bereavement may demand that you re-evaluate your current relationship needs, or it could be within existing relationships that your priorities are changing. It is important that you honour your own personal values while you include those of others around you.

We run into difficulties when we try to live up to others' expectations of us, or our own which have become out-of-date. The fear of failing to conform to peer pressure as a young person may cause us to anticipate feeling isolated and unloved. It is natural that we want the approval of those we love, respect or admire. But the price of that approval may be submerging our inner self and denying our inner strength.

Paradoxically perhaps, the truer we are to ourselves, the more we attract those relationships that are most nurturing and rewarding. The images of people we may think most desirable and appealing do not necessarily fulfil our companionship needs. In learning to be more accountable in our relationships, we realize that we are responsible for how we feel. No matter what is going on around us with other people, we can potentially choose to experience a positive emotion.

If we are feeling less than happy, we are responsible for being aware of it and for initiating the move towards regaining a happy state. 'Responsible' here means having the ability to respond, rather than carrying a burden. Restoring a happier frame of mind may involve asking for the assistance of one or more others.

When others around you are upset or emotionally disturbed in some way, you may choose to respond with empathy and compassion that is expressed from your own inner strength. It is up to you to maintain your inner level of loving because only you can know when you are depleted emotionally.

Acts of co-operating inwardly to respect or nurture yourself will enable you to respond outwardly as the occasions demand in your relationships with others. Giving yourself the permission, or freedom, to choose for yourself how you best honour what is true for you will provide a solid core of understanding and strength from which others can derive benefit.

The beauty of learning accountability and co-operation is that of beginning to get free from the attitude of *blaming*, with its destructive negative emotions, either yourself or anyone else for your current experiences. With a consciousness of understanding, you learn the lessons from your own past errors and freely choose the attitudes and actions that take you forward into the quality of relationships you would now most like to enjoy.

It was mentioned earlier that understanding can come about rather like switching on a light in the darkness (see Chapter 2). In the following guided visualization, you can envisage a light healing any hurt of a former misunderstanding. Pain is often a doorway to the opportunity of a greater experience of love.

Remember: Enough loving can heal all our differences . . .
What is *enough loving*? Loving, until it helps.

Turn on the Light of your Understanding

Choose a quiet place of solitude and make sure your body is resting comfortably . . . Breathe gently and deeply, cherishing each breath as it enters your body . . . Envisage the breath enriching you with loving, bringing you once again into contact with your inner wealth of peace . . . healing . . . and abundance . . .

Bring to mind an occasion when you were feeling upset or disappointed . . . Listen for any information that your feelings may have for you . . . What is it that you were feeling? Was it sadness? Was it grief? Was it frustration? What was the nature of your hurting? Let those feelings have their voice . . . What are they telling you? What is it they have to express to you?

Listen for the message . . . Be open to receive the healing available for you now . . . As you listen, imagine yourself walking into a mist of cleansing white light . . . See it sparkling around you . . . Feel its softness on your skin . . . As it touches you, notice a tingling as you come more alive within yourself . . . You may even hear sounds of the most soothing music somewhere in the distance . . .

In this light, you might imagine gifts of pure love being showered over you . . . All is clear . . . All is love . . . The darkness is dissolved . . . In this consciousness of understanding, there is only light . . . there is only love . . . And you find yourself at one . . . with yourself . . . and with all around you . . . Breathe in deeply and experience fully the light of your understanding . . . Feel the joy of knowing that

*you are protected and supported wherever you may be . . . Taste the
freedom and confidence of making the choices that most nurture
you . . . the choices that most fully enable you to give and receive
the best of yourself in all of your relationships . . . including that
most important one with yourself . . .*

*As you bring your awareness back into your present surroundings,
feel the warmth and reassurance in being just who you are right now.*

Look with Loving

In perhaps our worst moments, we can become so
consumed with an upset or opinion that it assumes a
certain 'reality' for us. What if the greater reality were
always the loving perspective we can choose for ourselves?
A natural by-product of a loving perspective is that of
understanding. With a loving perspective, we can see and
appreciate many points of view, many ways of leading life
that could be very different from our own.

What if we could greet each day with the equivalent of
'rose-coloured glasses', where the colour pink provided us
with a filter of loving reality for all our experiences? Through
such a filter, we could discern and co-operate with what is
true for us. At the same time, we would no longer suffer
from promoting negative emotions within or around us.

Understanding – with the Eyes of Loving

This is an exercise you can 'wear', an exercise in which you put on
a pair of glasses rather like sunglasses except that rather than dim
the light coming in to you, they enhance the light of your inner sight
– sunglasses in reverse.

You can put these glasses on for any time from, say, five minutes
to half a day or even the night-time when you are sleeping. Your
dreams can also be lifted with the light of your own loving.

With these glasses, your filter of perception is one of loving. When you look through them, you see in such a way that you feel a quality of inner expansion, beauty, empathy, peace, humour, laughter, compassion, bliss, whatever way you might identify the inner experience of loving. If you need to take a firm stand with someone, and sound angry perhaps, you might entertain the feeling of joy within you at the same time, and hold the vision of loving throughout for yourself and the other person.

Now try and see for yourself. Take at least ten minutes today as an experiment to wear your filters of loving vision.

Peace . . . Becoming a Friend to Yourself (I) and Others (O)

The quality of peace proposed in *Superlove* is one that emanates from intuitive understanding and acceptance of ourselves and others. As already discussed, it is not merely passive, in the sense of an absence of conflict, but much more active. The happiness produced by the inner knowing that all is right in your world **(I)** results in a healthy vitality that naturally seeks loving expression and is available for achievement outwardly **(O)**.

Your peace is within you and it is within your capacity to discover it. By nurturing moments of awareness of your peace, the picture will gradually grow inside you. Like almost anything else, the experience will come as you direct your attention towards it more and more.

This inner experience of peace is the result of working with loving understanding when you meet anything that might represent conflict to you. Life is, of course, full of conflict. Yet it is possible, with an attitude of acceptance, to redirect and use the energy of conflict to fulfil a peaceful positive purpose. Inwardly, we can use the awareness of an upset or emotional disturbance to make a fresh choice.

Are you fully grateful for the gift of your life? Perhaps it is only when we fully come into contact with, know and relate to the peace within us that we can truly say we are grateful, and indeed, gratefully receiving, the gift of our life.

Peace – Gratefully Receiving the Gift of your Life

This is a very simple exercise that you can practise in any spare moment to nurture your peace and awaken to the gift of your life. To begin with, you may require an external stimulant or reflector to take you into an inner moment of peace. For example, is there a piece of music, a painting, the scent of a particular flower, a certain birdsong, a view, or a favourite animal that specially touches, warms or lifts you into a sense of greater well-being? Is there somewhere you can go that takes you into the indefinable quality of your own tenderness or sensitivity? What can you bring to mind that makes you feel calm, quiet and at one with yourself? It could be a memory of some event, person or experience.

All you need to do for this exercise is to set a few minutes aside to focus on your peace. Choose something to do, inwardly or outwardly, to promote your experience of peace.

When you have created that experience, enjoy fully that moment within yourself. Let go of any attention to anything outside you now.

While you are in touch with your own sense of being, take a pen and paper and complete the following sentence as many times as ideas pop into your mind:

I am gratefully receiving the gift of...................in my life.

This could look like:

♥ I am gratefully receiving the gift of stillness in my life.
♥ I am gratefully receiving the gift of loving in my life.

♥ I am gratefully receiving the gift of nature in my life.
♥ I am gratefully receiving the gift of freedom in my life.
♥ I am gratefully receiving the gift of fun in my life.

The exercise could look quite different for you, so just allow yourself
to respond spontaneously with whatever comes up. You may be
surprised at what you discover. Within the storehouse of your life
are more gifts than you could ever imagine. As you learn to receive,
you can also share them and create the space for more to come to
you.

   This makes relating with others a simple and joyful adventure of
increasing value.

Peace that Grows from the Inside (I)
Out (O)

It is a radical approach for many of us to think about
inwardly nurturing ourselves (I) first, so that we may
contribute to others (O) with loving insight and awareness.
You might imagine what might be your own expectations
of a good friend. Then think about how you could begin
extending those qualities into greater friendship towards
yourself. You might, for example, be less demanding, more
patient, forgiving, considerate and light-hearted.

   As you inwardly open a greater channel for receiving
friendship (I), you may well attract more of the friends (O)
who best support you and in whose company you have the
most fun. Once you have *experienced* how nurturing
yourself first does in fact enhance your capacity for
enjoying more fulfilling relationships, this idea may make
more sense to you.

   It is worth remembering that it is perhaps only when
we *give* of what we have within us that we do in fact truly
receive it.

Give (O) – and Receive (I) your Peace

Do not believe for one moment the saying 'Opportunity only knocks once.' It does not! If you are open for it, opportunities can just about knock you over as they keep presenting themselves to you.

Look back over the last Peace exercise and recall one of the gifts you received. Once again, bring it vividly into your imagination until you can fully re-experience it.

Now take a few moments and bring to mind that one person, or perhaps group of people, who might benefit from your gift. It could be an elderly neighbour, orphaned children in care, your mother or father, a work colleague experiencing bereavement, a teenager at odds with his parents or your own children. This exercise is to set aside at least ten minutes to be **(I)** and give **(O)** of yourself, however you are inwardly prompted to express this.

This kind of giving may take you beyond rules, expectations and former conditions concerning love in action. Be open to the giving taking many forms. For example, you could communicate the gift through your eyes, without ever saying a word. You could pick up the phone, and share your gift by listening. You might write a letter of appreciation.

Your purpose here is to bring about the attunement with an inner gift and in a simple and easy manner, give it away to one or more others. Observe and notice how in the simplest acts of giving your sense of peace and well-being become enhanced.

Expansion . . . Winning in All Ways

The time to consider expansion might be the point at which you are tempted to 'contract' away from your sources of loving **(I) + (O)**. When we contract away from our loving, it is often out of anger, with its motivation for fight, or out of fear, with its motivation for flight. Both anger and fear, fight and flight, reflect the *lack of contact* with our loving, the uncertainty or *doubt* that we have about *ourselves*.

This doubt often occurs during periods of transition or change in our lives, such as retirement, redundancy, divorce and even sometimes, marriage or the arrival of a new baby in the family. Irrational emotions often flare up in ways that make no sense. It is especially at these times that we are called upon to extend greater acceptance and understanding towards ourselves, nurturing our inner peace, so that we can fully embrace the opportunities for expansion.

Those incidents of uncertainty, when we are prompted to withdraw or withhold our participation in our relationships, or to strike out in anger in the vain attempt to change something we do not like, are revealing to us opportunities for self-healing. Self-healing is first of all acknowledging that you are emotionally out of balance, and secondly, admitting that you need to receive love, tolerance, support and even assistance or guidance from others.

To admit **(I)** to your vulnerability and need as a human being may open the doors to expanding your capacity **(O)** for loving others. When you are truly receptive and sensitive **(I)** to your own deepest concerns, you will attune to the deepest concerns **(O)** in others.

Expansion – The Path of Least Resistance

The *Triangle of Trust* is an approach to self-healing that leads towards greater loving in your relationships. The steps are simply as follows:

1. **Doubt** – The Absence of Loving
   When you experience negative emotion, it is a call for you to direct some of your loving attention to balance the disturbance you are experiencing.
2. **Discipline** – Attune to your Loving
   Forgive yourself for any thoughts, words or actions you

may have held against yourself or others. Let go of your attachments to any negative conditions. Refocus your attention on the positive opportunities being presented to you.

3. **Fun** – Take the Path of Least Resistance
   Build a foundation of appreciation and *gratitude* for yourself and those concerned. Look for the signs of *humour* and enjoyment, even in unlikely times and places. Take small steps to approach your challenges with loving *enthusiasm*. Prepare to *celebrate* your newfound capacities for loving **(I) + (O)**.

Expanding through Effective Communication

Expansion is a natural extension of loving **(I) > (O) > (I)** that comes from the inner world of strength that you have created through greater self-acceptance, understanding and peacefulness. We all have a need to express ourselves, especially towards those who are important to us, and have also, perhaps equally, a need to be heard by them. The form of our loving expression may be 'receptive' as we listen, or more 'pro-active' as we talk.

Communication boils down to the need to pay attention and *listen* to ourselves inwardly, then offering that skill of attentive listening to others. In talking we need to remember (as much as we can) to *speak kind words* to ourselves and others. Even the most difficult communications can be made in kindness, and may be more effective when they are.

Rejoice . . . It's a Wonderful Life

Imagine yourself in the world with fresh eyes, seeing with openness and curiosity the rich variety of ways in which your fellow human beings organize, and sometimes disorganize, themselves. There is great humour being played out and yet you may not always perceive it as such. If you have lost the sight and sound of divine laughter, you may have dropped beneath the level of that awareness.

It is potentially within the capacity of your loving to lift yourself above the cares and concerns which may have held you down. You may reach a hand up to a person closer to that loving source of enthusiasm and allow them to lift you into a higher perspective. For this to work, you must initially be willing to make the first move, to receive the gift being offered and then carry on up once you have overcome your inertia.

Alternatively, you may reach your hand to someone also in need of encouragement. As you share inspiration with that other person, you also receive for yourself, and the sum total can be greater joy, vitality and delight for both of you.

If happiness is not happening for you in the way you would like, you do have at least these two options. You can turn and give something of yourself to another person who is there to receive. Or, when in need yourself, you can turn to another, ask and receive.

When you look around you, from a loving perspective **(I)**, you will notice many instances of the gentle triumph of loving over the many challenges to it **(O)**. You will become more aware of them **(O)** as you learn to develop greater attunement to your own gentle, or not so gentle, loving conquests **(I)** of negative patterns or attitudes.

How we perceive relationships, especially those most significant for us, is a reflection of how we perceive certain aspects of ourselves. When positively experienced, we can direct our loving to amplify those relationships. When relationships are experienced negatively, we can direct our loving to bring about healing, **(I)** and/or **(O)**.

The great key is remembering to re-attune to the loving

within you when it has gone out of focus. At its deepest level, your loving will incorporate bliss, expansiveness, peace, union with all life forms, inner light or quiet contentment. In this next exercise, you will have the opportunity of discovering the symbol that most represents that quality of loving within you. This symbol can be like a 'hot line' to your central sources of loving, a reminder to you of your greatest asset.

Your Gift from the Child Within

You will need a pen and paper for this exercise, so have these ready. Take the next few moments to be quiet and reflective within yourself. You might like to make physical contact with your Inner Child by placing your hand on your abdomen. Feel the warmth and reassurance coming from your hands.

Bring to your mind an experience of loving that brought a quality of exuberance or joy to you. It could have been a quiet moment shared with a loved one . . . a time of celebration . . . a surprise gift of loving – received or given . . .

What was that supreme quality of loving that you experienced? Was it joy, harmony, bliss, ecstasy, peace, contentment . . .?

When you have identified that greatest quality, draw it in symbolic form in as much detail or as simply as you would like.

For example:

Figure 14: Quality: *Enthusiasm*

Now explore the following questions relating to your symbol:

1. What does the symbol mean for you? *(This may go beyond the quality it initially represented for you.)*
2. What action(s) can you take to *express* that meaning more fully in your life and in your relationships, **(I)** + **(O)**?
3. What action(s) can you take to *experience* that meaning more fully in your life and in your relationships, **(I)** + **(O)**?
4. What other information does the symbol have to give you about amplifying your sources of loving?
5. What action, **(I)** or **(O)**, will you take in the next ten minutes to demonstrate the meaning of your symbol?

For example:
1. I feel sunny and smiling and tingling with happiness.
2. I can phone my friend who is feeling glum and arrange to take her out for a treat.
3. I can stick the symbol up in my office to remind me of that quality when I have difficult phone calls to make.
4. Simply smiling (even when I do not feel like it) makes me feel happier and more loving and helps whoever I am with to feel better also.
5. I will smile, and enjoy the next ten minutes of happy thoughts.

Walking Blessings

What if each of us are blessings in disguise? We often disguise ourselves, clothing the essence of ourselves to get attention, approval and love from those we value and care about. A turning-point in our development can be when we encounter those, often those closest to us, who erode our superficial presentation, or form. In such a case, we can fight and resist the challenge they present to us, or we can (more wisely) recognize this as a point of expansion, an opportunity to grow, experience and present ourselves in ways that our more authentic or true.

Those who would challenge your form of expression *bring* you a blessing in disguise. It may be through a row or feelings of personal rejection or any other negative experience that you *become aware* of the shortfall between the loving that you are and the means you have been using to communicate it. Once you are aware of this, you can recognize and appreciate the blessing being brought by the one who challenged you. You can further extend the blessing of your own goodwill to whoever offended you.

What if, in all life forms, especially the human ones, a powerful and positive purpose is being enacted? A loving purpose: for us all to learn how we can utilize the blessings we embody to the greatest benefit of all. As we refine ourselves to attune positively to all aspects within us, we gain greater understanding and generosity towards those others we encounter – until we arrive at the point at which we can honestly say that we do love life . . . in all of its forms.

Raindrops
I treasure the rain sometimes
Because I must stay inside
Looking out
I see like precious jewels
Raindrops
Strung like pearls
Along the balcony railings.

However stormy outside
I can always return,
Look in,
Be – in my still,
Warm centre
Of peacefulness.

> The weather may be
> Beyond my control.
> Where I look –
> That's always up to me.

You, and those important to you, are naturally endowed with many seeds of happiness. Loving is the choice you make to nurture those seeds. Opportunities abound to choose the positive option, to become one with the loving that you are and to enrich your life with happiness.

Dear Reader,

I hope that through reading *Superlove*,
you will discover how the power of your loving
can enrich both you and those with whom you interact.
Above all, I hope that you find it easier to accept
and appreciate yourself and others more fully.

My request to you is that if you enjoy reading *Superlove* –

tell your friends!

Miracles do not necessarily happen overnight.
Remember to be patient with yourself.

When you start observing how *Superlove*
is making a difference in your life and your relationships,
please drop me a line, c/o Thorsons.

Index

action 43, 76–8, 123ff
acts of loving 177–9

barricades 96–115
  breaking down 116–49
blessings 196–8
breathing for peace 92–5
bridges
  inner 58–61
  in relationships 56–8

care of self 45–7
change 41, 75, *see also* actions
childlike vs childish 180–1
communication 56–7, 61–2, 123–4,
    127, 193
compensation 156
confidence 123ff
conflict 83–4, 127ff

deletion 61
denial 151–2
discipline 68, 133–4, 192
distortion 61
doubt 124–9, 192
dreams 158–64
  fulfilling 158–9

endurance 153
expansion (of self) 116–49, 191–3

Fairy Godparent 165–8
forgiveness 104–9, 134–5, 135–7
  statements of 109–10

fun 68–9, 115, 144, 147ff, 153, 192

generalization 61
gratitude 123ff, 148
guardian angels 164–5
guilt 99–104
  freedom from 101–4

happiness 19–20, 40–4
healing 123ff
heroes 28–9
hurt 51–4

imagination 154–8
inner child 36–40, 67–75, 86, 123,
    150–80, 180–9, 196
  loving 69–71
  relating to 37–40
  setting free 179
  understanding 67–8
inspirational self 34–6, 75, 86
integration 123ff
intuition 172–3

knowing what you want 164

language 61–2
laughter 147ff, *see also* light touch
learning 123ff
light touch 148–9
love 40–1, 180–98
  looking with 187–8

magic 155–7, 167–8

negative
  feeling 128
  sacrificing the 141–2
  thinking 107–8
nurturing 68, 127–9

observation 182–4
opinion 62

parenthood 137–8, 150ff
patience 153
peace 83–115, 188–91
  meaning of 84–5
  peace cycle 90–2
  positive 85–6
perspective 71–5
positive orientation 26–8, 142–3
projection 62

rejoice 194–6
relationship
  authentic 138–40
  with others 56–61, 118ff
  with yourself 20–1ff, 33–40,
    138–40

resentment 99–104
  freedom from 101–4
revenge 117

self-acceptance 19–46, 47–82, 181–2
  accepting the facts 25–6
  demonstration of 30–3
  first steps 23–4
  positive orientation 26–7
  and understanding 47–82
self-awareness 21–2
self-righteousness 117–18
speculation 62
support 153

treatfeast 170–2
time 127–9
touch 56–7
Triangle of Trust 68–9, 125–6, 144

understanding 47–82, 184–6, 186–7
  first steps 50–1

vulnerability 129

Of further interest . . .

Superlife

The seven steps that spell S.U.C.C.E.S.S.

Anne Naylor

Superlife is an astonishingly simple 7-step approach that will help you find out what it is that you really want out of life, clarify your thoughts and actions, build up confidence and inner power, and achieve success in everything you do.

★ Set Personal Objectives
★ Unlock your Attitude
★ Clear Away Blocks
★ Create Inner Strength
★ Expect Success
★ Simply Have Fun
★ Start Now!

Superlife is a straightforward guide to personal accountability, choice and freedom. It is full of wit and wisdom, and a practical and inspiring companion for you on your path towards a fulfilling, successful new life.

Anne Naylor has developed a unique motivational and personal growth programme which she teaches both in the UK and the US. She has discovered through this work that everyone has an inbuilt 'success mechanism' which it *is* possible to activate!

You Can't Afford the Luxury of a Negative Thought

A book for people with any life-threatening illness – including life!

John-Roger and Peter McWilliams

Negative thinking can damage your health!

It is one of the most serious diseases of our time, obstructing us from believing that we really *deserve* happiness: an attitude which affects us mentally, physically and emotionally. Negative thinking can provide the right environment for illness to prosper. How important it is, then, for those with serious illnesses *not* to indulge in it.

The cure is simple. *Savour* the positive in your life; weed out the negative; *enjoy* each moment. The path is not easy but this best-selling book will infect you with its sense of fun and its gregarious wisdom. Packed with inspirational quotes, it will unlock new possibilities in your life as well as being both compelling and uplifting reading. Accept *your* right to live life to the full!

'A work of unique simplicity which offers a way of thinking and living in which motives are high but realistic and available. I love it.' – Pauline Collins

Life 101

Everything we wished we had learned about life in school – but didn't

John-Roger and Peter McWilliams

In all the time you spent at school, you probably never learned the *really* useful things – the things you actually wanted to know.

For example: did you learn what your purpose in life was? You probably weren't taught how to deal with guilt, pain and fear, or were shown how hurt can lead to learning and personal growth. It's unlikely that you were told about the value of mistakes, or the importance of acceptance as a first step in changing things for the better. And there probably weren't any classes on anger, depression, confusion or forgiveness.

In short, you didn't learn much about *life*. The good news is that it's never too late, or too early, to begin to learn all the things you weren't taught at school.

You are the teacher; you choose yourself what you want to learn. This book is full of practical suggestions for living your life. Open it and find out the things you *should* have been taught at school.

John-Roger and Peter McWilliams are the authors of the bestselling books, *You Can't Afford the Luxury of a Negative Thought, Do It! A Guide to Living your Dreams* and *Wealth 101*.

'Advice about the human condition' – *New York Times*

Wealth 101

Getting what you want –
enjoying what you've got

John-Roger and Peter McWilliams

This is not a book on investing cleverly so you can retire to Florida in two years. This book goes beyond get-rich-quick schemes. It even goes beyond money. It is about *wealth*.

What is Wealth?
The authors define wealth as health, happiness, abundance, prosperity, riches, loving, caring, sharing, learning, knowing what we want, opportunity, enjoying and balance.

Wealth 101 explores, in detail, how to enjoy the life you already have. Then, with appreciation and gratitude, how to obtain more of what you really want. And finally, achieving a balance between getting what you want and enjoying what you've got.

Wealth 101, like the authors' previous books – all of which have reached No. 1 on the *New York Times* bestseller list – is a joy to read, full of fun, wit and wisdom. It will show you the riches in your life you didn't know you possessed.

Do It!

A guide to living your dreams

John-Roger and Peter McWilliams

Stop making excuses!
We all cherish at least one dream – a heart's desire.
Moreover, it is a fact that most of us do have the time and
the ability to fulfil our dreams – if we put our mind to it.
Unfortunately, we spend all our precious time and energy
on other things, often completely unrelated to what we
really want to do. What is it that makes us procrastinate?

The answer is the comfort zone – the old, safe, practised
thoughts, responses and actions we feel comfortable with.
Pursuing a dream involves ways of thinking and acting that
are outside the boundaries of this comfort zone. But how
can we overcome such a problem when we probably aren't
even aware that it exists!

This book provides the answer.

- recognize your comfort zone and learn to go beyond it
- discover, or rediscover, your dreams
- choose which dreams to pursue
- work out practical solutions for achieving them

As the authors say, 'LET'S GET OFF OUR "BUTS".'
So stop making excuses, and start living your dreams!

SUPERLIFE	0 7225 2600 8	£4.99	☐
YOU CAN'T AFFORD THE LUXURY			
OF A NEGATIVE THOUGHT	0 7225 2383 1	£8.99	☐
LIFE 101	0 7225 2696 2	£7.99	☐
WEALTH 101	0 7225 2855 8	£8.99	☐
DO IT!	0 7225 2695 4	£7.99	☐

All these books are available from your local bookseller or can be ordered direct from the publishers.

To order direct just tick the titles you want and fill in the form below:

Name: _____

Address: _____

_____

_____ Postcode:_____

Send to: Thorsons Mail Order, Dept 3, HarperCollins*Publishers*, Westerhill Road, Bishopbriggs, Glasgow G64 2QT.
Please enclose a cheque or postal order or your authority to debit your Visa/Access account —

Credit card no: _____

Expiry date: _____

Signature: _____

— up to the value of the cover price plus:
UK & BFPO: Add £1.00 for the first book and 25p for each additional book ordered.
Overseas orders including Eire: Please add £2.95 service charge. Books will be sent by surface mail but quotes for airmail despatches will be given on request.

24 HOUR TELEPHONE ORDERING SERVICE FOR ACCESS/VISA CARDHOLDERS — TEL: **041 772 2281.**